Living Faith

Living Faith

Through the Church's Year

STEPHEN W. NEED

RESOURCE *Publications* • Eugene, Oregon

LIVING FAITH
Through the Church's Year

Copyright © 2020 Stephen W. Need. All rights reserved. Except for brief quotations in critical publications or reviews, no part of this book may be reproduced in any manner without prior written permission from the publisher. Write: Permissions, Wipf and Stock Publishers, 199 W. 8th Ave., Suite 3, Eugene, OR 97401.

Resource Publications
An Imprint of Wipf and Stock Publishers
199 W. 8th Ave., Suite 3
Eugene, OR 97401

www.wipfandstock.com

PAPERBACK ISBN: 978-1-7252-5517-3
HARDCOVER ISBN: 978-1-7252-5518-0
EBOOK ISBN: 978-1-7252-5519-7

Manufactured in the U.S.A.   03/10/20

All biblical quotations, unless otherwise noted, are from the NRSV.

for Simon

Contents

Abbreviations	x
Introduction	xiii
PART 1: THROUGH THE CHURCH'S YEAR	1
1. Advent	3
Big Bang: The Universe in Motion	3
Imago Dei: The Image of God	6
Desert: The Sound of Sheer Silence	9
Justice: The Color Purple	12
Messengers from God: Be an Angel!	15
2. Christmas and Epiphany	18
Bethlehem: The Stooping of God	18
In a Manger: The Christmas Crib	21
Messiah: Jesus' Godly Life	23
Epiphany: "Sonic Light"	26
Baptism: Redrawing the Boundaries	29
3. Lent, Easter, and Ascension	33
Ash Wednesday: T. S. Eliot's Journey	33
Lent (I): The Integrity of Job	36
Lent (II): Abiding	39
Lent (III): The Rich Fool	41

Palm Sunday: Joining in the Story	44
The Last Supper: Who Are We?	47
Good Friday (I): The Kelham Rood	50
Good Friday (II): *Night*	53
Good Friday (III): Jesus the Lamb of God	56
Holy Saturday: Holy Fire!	58
Easter Day: The Garden of God	61
Ascension Day: Don't Cling to Me	64

4. Pentecost and Trinity — 68

Paraclete: Tested in the Fire	68
Pentecost: El Greco	71
Triunity: The Triangular Lodge	74
Trinity Sunday: God's Two Hands	77

Part 2: Living Faith — 81

1. Jesus — 83

Caesarea Philippi: Jesus the Turning Point	83
The Samaritan Woman: Jesus the Water of Life	86
Stilling the Storm: Jesus and the Chaos	89
Speaking Out: Jesus the Prophet	91
People and Places: Jesus the New Temple	94

2. The Saints — 98

Mary: Seat of Wisdom	98
The Curé d'Ars: Humility and Simplicity	101
St. Benedict: Prayer and Work	104
St. Dominic: Preaching and Teaching	106
St. Francis: Theology and Ecology	109

3. Christian Faith — 113

Cheley Park: God in Nature	113
Food and Drink: Metaphors of Divine Life	116
Personal Mark: A Sense of Mystery	119
Bach and the Mustard Seed: The Promise of the Kingdom	121
C. S. Lewis and St. Paul: God's Self-Giving Love	125
First and Second Corinthians: Strength and Weakness	127
The Fish: Resurrection Journey	130
Patmos: The New Creation	133

4. Christian Life   **137**

Ephphatha: Be Opened!   137
Paddington Bear: A New Family   140
Bridges over Troubled Waters: Reconciliation   143
Mother Teresa: Small Things with Great Love   146
Jesus Wept: Crying and Salvation   148
Jesus' Prayer Book: Praying with the Psalms   151
Be'er Sheva: Doing Justice   154
The Last Things: Work in Progress   157

Afterword   **161**

Bibliography   **163**

Abbreviations

Gen	Genesis
Exod	Exodus
Lev	Leviticus
Num	Numbers
Deut	Deuteronomy
Josh	Joshua
Judg	Judges
1 Sam	1 Samuel
2 Sam	2 Samuel
1 Kgs	1 Kings
2 Kgs	2 Kings
1 Chr	1 Chronicles
2 Chr	2 Chronicles
Neh	Nehemiah
Ps	Psalm
Prov	Proverbs
Isa	Isaiah
Jer	Jeremiah
Lam	Lamentations
Ezek	Ezekiel
Dan	Daniel
Hos	Hosea
Zech	Zechariah
Mal	Malachi

Tob	Tobit
Matt	Matthew
Rom	Romans
1 Cor	1 Corinthians
2 Cor	2 Corinthians
Gal	Galatians
Eph	Ephesians
Phil	Philippians
Col	Colossians
1 Thess	1 Thessalonians
2 Thess	2 Thessalonians
1 Tim	1 Timothy
Heb	Hebrews
Jas	James
1 Pet	1 Peter
2 Pet	2 Peter
Rev	Revelation
KJV	King James Version / Authorised Version
RSV	Revised Standard Version
NRSV	New Revised Standard Version
NEB	New English Bible
JB	Jerusalem Bible

Introduction

Living Faith: Through the Church's Year is designed to meet an immediate practical need. Very often those who preach, teach or lead Bible studies need a short, easily accessible article to read in a limited time and to use as a basis for their sermon or session. Each of the short reflections included here provides exactly that. But the book can also be used by individuals for private study or meditation. Directions for further study and discussion include Bible references, questions, and further reading, either for group work or individually at home. Each piece is a stand-alone study and opens with an illustration such as a well-known painting, piece of music, sculpture, building or text. Hopefully whoever you are and wherever you are, you will find these pieces lively, accessible, insightful, and helpful.

The book is divided into two parts. Part 1 follows the basic outline of the church's year. An opening Advent reflection on the big bang suggests that God comes to us in the movement of creation. Further Advent pieces address other ways in which we experience God: through his image within us, in the desert, through justice, and through each other. In the Christmas and Epiphany section the focus is on God coming to us in the birth and life of Jesus, through music and in a new lifestyle. For Lent, Easter, and Ascension there are reflections on Job, the Kelham Rood, and the Garden of God. For Pentecost and Trinity, the Holy Paraclete, a curious trinitarian building in Northamptonshire, England, and God's "two hands" are included.

The pieces in part 2 are about the life of faith and can be used at any time. They are divided into four sections: first, "Jesus"—including a look at Jesus the water of life, and Jesus the new temple; second, "Saints"—with a look at Mary and Benedict, among others; third, "Christian Faith"—focusing on aspects of belief such as God in nature and the resurrection journey; and finally, "Christian Life"—with an emphasis on practical matters such as Jesus' new family, praying with the psalms, and the place of the Last Things.

The pieces included here are written from a theological stance characterized by three very important dimensions: the "living-moving world," the "living-moving text," and our "living-moving faith." This perspective experiences creation as living and moving. The world is not static or finished but always alive and developing. It's an organism which God permeates in bursts of expanding creativity. The text of the Bible is also living and moving, not static and finished but continually being reimagined in new and changing contexts, yielding new insights and depths of meaning. And finally, our faith isn't static or finished. It is also moving, evolving, and developing as we find new layers of meaning and insight that carry us forward into deeper understanding of Christian discipleship.

Living Faith can be used in many different ways and could be accompanied by appropriate PowerPoint presentations of the painting, place or item concerned, listening to the selected music or reading the relevant text. The potential for growth in faith is enormous.

Wherever you find yourself using this book, I hope it will provide challenging insights and enable creative reflections leading to new horizons and lively faith.

All quotations from the Bible are from the New Revised Standard Version unless otherwise noted. I would like to thank the staff at Resource Publications for their encouragement in bringing this book to completion and Meg Booth for helping me with American spellings and punctuation. Any weaknesses are, of course, my own.

Stephen W. Need
Essex, England
November 2019

PART 1

Through the Church's Year

1

Advent

BIG BANG: THE UNIVERSE IN MOTION

JUST ABOUT EVERYBODY THESE days has heard of the "big bang." People might not be able to explain it but they've usually at least heard of it. The big bang is the theory about the beginning of the universe held by most scientists today. And it's so much part of the contemporary understanding of the way things began that most people now take it for granted.

Proposed originally as a "cosmic egg" theory by a Roman Catholic priest called Georges Lemaître in the 1930s, it now goes something like this: about 13.8 billion years ago there was an enormous explosion of matter at a very high temperature. This explosion started off a process of movement and expansion which included the emergence of ripples throughout the universe. These are still discernible today. Gradually, over the next several billion years, protons, neutrons, and electrons emerged. Then atoms were shaped, followed by stars and galaxies. Carbon was formed in the stars and eventually life on earth emerged. People argue about exactly what happened next but the key idea is "motion": the whole place is in a constant state of "motion." The well-known English theoretical physicist and cosmologist Stephen Hawking describes some of these ideas in his popular writing for non-scientists.[1]

Other developments in modern science and anthropology give the same message: the world is moving. The theory of evolution, stemming from Charles Darwin in the nineteenth century, is based on the observation that forms of life on earth are constantly evolving. Darwin published

---

1. See esp. Hawking, *Brief History*, and the more recent *Brief Answers*.

PART 1: THROUGH THE CHURCH'S YEAR

the findings from his Beagle Voyage journey in a famous book in which he explained his theory of "evolution by natural selection."[2] Life on earth emerged about four million years ago and human life about two hundred thousand years ago. It then developed from one state to another, gradually evolving. There are different interpretations of Darwin but few now doubt that human life is in a constant state of motion, change, growth, and development.

The same general principle is clear from quantum physics or quantum mechanics. Emanating from the work of Max Planck (1858–1947), this examines the world at the subatomic level observing that the basic substance of the universe is energy rather than static blocks. Common sense may tell us that things are static but actually they're not: at the subatomic level everything is moving. Indeed, the word *quanta* refers to packets of energy. Once again, following this view, motion is fundamental to the way the world is. Related ideas such as Einstein's theory of relativity and Hubble's "expanding universe" reinforce this basic sense of motion and movement.

From these key developments in modern thinking, it can be seen that at three important levels (the macro level of the big bang, the intermediate level of human life, and the micro level of quantum mechanics) everything can be seen to be in motion. The universe is a moving organism, a stream of energy constantly evolving and expanding from an initial explosion.

For many people, though not all, this reading of the origins of the universe is in conflict with the accounts of creation in the book of Genesis. But whatever we think about that, it is clear that Genesis also emphasizes movement in God's process of creation. There are two accounts of creation in Genesis, the first in chapter 1 and the second in chapter 2. Genesis 1 consists of the various days of creation. The opening words are usually translated, "In the beginning God created . . ."[3] but the Hebrew is probably better translated, "When God began to create . . ."[4] This rendering indicates the beginning of a process. Then, the various days are numbered and the parts of creation identified: light on the first day; the firmament on the second day; the vegetation, plants, and trees on the third day; day, night, and the stars on the fourth day; living creatures, birds, and sea monsters on the fifth day; and beasts of the earth, cattle, and human beings on the sixth day. The

2. Darwin, *Origin*.
3. E.g., the KJV, the RSV, and the JB.
4. See the footnotes to Gen 1:1 in Meeks, *HarperCollins Study Bible*.

4

seventh day is the day of rest (2:1–3). The account in Genesis 2 differs in a number of ways. Instead of focusing on the creation of the world including man and woman, it focuses on the creation of human life, first of Adam and then of Eve taken out of Adam's side. In both accounts, creation takes time: it's not a single act of creation by fiat. Similar ideas of God's creative process can be found in the book of Isaiah (e.g., 40:12; 41:17–20; 42:14–17).

And it's interesting that from the very beginning Christians have seen connections between Christ and creation, emphasizing that in Christ the whole universe has taken another turn in its development. So, St. Paul speaks of Christ as "the firstborn of all creation" (Col 1:15–20) and of the "new creation" in Christ (2 Cor 5:17; Gal 6:15; cf. Col 3:10). There's a strong sense here that Christ is part of God's movement in creation as he turns it onward toward its final perfection.

One of the most important things for understanding and living Christian faith today is that we see the world as it really is: moving. Creation is a living, moving, changing, developing organism still on its way to completion.[5] The world is not a machine that operates rigidly without change. It's God's moving organism—more like a plant than a clock. And human beings are immersed within it, changing and developing as it grows. The realization that the creation is in constant motion helps make a good deal of sense of a lot of Christian doctrine and belief. As God moves in creating the world, so creation moves with God who is creating at every moment. God comes to us in the movement of creation as it expands, develops, and recreates. The world is not a finished project; there are still things to be perfected. Things still go wrong but the process is oriented to completion by the end of time.

The big bang, evolution, quantum physics, the book of Genesis, and Jesus Christ himself all remind us of this one fundamental truth: that the whole creation is moving and growing toward God's final purpose for it at the end of time. And God comes to us repeatedly and in different ways in that continually moving and expanding creative process.

---

5. For a very stimulating visual experience of the universe illustrating movement, see Cox, *Planets*.

Part 1: Through the Church's Year

Bible Study Passages

Gen 1:1–25

Isa 40:12–23

Col 1:15–20

Questions for Discussion

Where and when have you noticed that the universe is "in motion"?

How would you interpret the accounts of creation in Genesis?

How, for you, are science and religion related?

What does it mean to say that Christ and creation are connected?

What is meant by creation "being perfected"?

Further Reading

Goldingay, John. *Genesis for Everyone*. Part 1. Chs. 1–16. London: SPCK, 2010.

Holder, Rodney. *Big Bang, Big God: A Universe Designed for Life?* London: Lion, 2013.

IMAGO DEI: THE IMAGE OF GOD

If you stand in the Sistine Chapel in the Vatican in Rome and look up at the ceiling, you'll be looking at the famous painting by Michelangelo. In a series of nine scenes from the book of Genesis depicting the creation of the world, the most striking is surely the *Creation of Adam* depicting God creating the first human being. The tantalizing scene depicts God, an old man with a beard, sitting inside what looks like a cosmic brain full of other creatures, and reaching out toward a youthful and naked Adam lying in a reclining position on a blue and green background. Their two hands nearly meet at the forefinger tips. This is the most famous moment in the whole painting. Adam seems to be complete and just setting off on an independent journey. Whether the closeness of the fingers suggests continuity or difference is debatable. Perhaps it's somehow both. In essence, the painting depicts the beginnings of creation.

Commissioned by Pope Julius II, the Sistine Chapel ceiling was painted by Michelangelo during the four years between 1508 and 1512. The chapel itself is named after Sixtus IV, who restored it. The painting was done before the other famous piece behind the High Altar: *The Last Judgment*. The ceiling and the High Altar background point to the beginning and the end, creation and judgment. The *Creation of Adam* has come to sum up the whole ceiling painting. It evokes the subtle and complex relation between humanity and God, and reflects the entire Christian theological tradition regarding humanity's relation to God, both in the beginning and since. The two fingers almost touching have become iconic in art and in imagination. Used and reused, interpreted and reinterpreted, the painting is comparable in terms of fame to Da Vinci's *Mona Lisa*.

How are we to think of the relation between God and humanity? What does the book of Genesis say? Certainly, God is creator. Then, the first thing we're told about human beings is that they're made in God's image: "Let us make humankind in our image, according to our likeness" (1:26). And then, "So God created humankind in his image, in the image of God he created them; male and female he created them" (1:27). In Genesis 5:1, when referring to Adam's descendants, we're told that God created humankind "in the likeness of God." And in Genesis 9:6, following the narrative about Noah and the flood, we're reminded that God made humankind "in his own image." In mainstream Christian thinking in the West, this image was lost in the fall of man when Adam and Eve ate the fruit of the tree of knowledge of good and evil and were cast out of the garden (Gen 3). Two important questions arise in all this: what exactly is the "image" of God? It is often stated confidently that like Adam, "we are all made in the image of God" but it is hard to say what that image is. And second, are we to think of the image and likeness of God as completely lost in the fall?

Theologians differ in their answers to these questions. Is the image our rational faculty, our capacity for self-reflection and consciousness? Is it our spiritual superiority or perhaps our moral consciousness? All these mark us out as different from other animals. Is it a creative capacity or a personal ability in relating to God? Perhaps, using all these ideas, the image could be seen as humankind's capacity for a special relation to God. If it is the combination of all these elements that raises us above the rest of creation and makes us like God, then what is lost in the so-called fall? For some the entire image was lost when Adam ate the fruit in the garden. Indeed, this is the view taken by St. Augustine (354–430) and the majority of Western thinkers. But there has been at least one other way of thinking of these things which makes a great deal of sense.

St. Irenaeus (ca. 130–ca. 200 CE), bishop of Lyons in the second century, pointed out that Genesis 1:26 refers to "image" and "likeness." Unlike the usual interpretation of the Genesis story, Irenaeus held that human beings were created in a state of childlike innocence rather than perfection. The fall for him was then an example of the many falls that human beings make along their journey through life. We were created innocent, in the image and likeness, but in the fall we lost the likeness while keeping the basic image. This means that instead of starting out perfect and then falling and being saved by Christ, we were created innocent and then grow toward the likeness which we lost. Irenaeus's view sees Christ, himself the image of God (2 Cor 4:4; Col 1:15; cf. Heb 1:3), not as one who simply reverts the process of the fall, but as one who gathers up or "recapitulates" everyone, restoring the process of likeness, and moving us on toward the end of time when we will be once again in the image and likeness. This process is much like the "divinization" or *theosis* (2 Pet 1:4) so important in eastern Christianity.

The famous painting by Michelangelo in the Sistine Chapel in Rome focuses on the two finger tips of God and Adam. There's a connection and yet also a distinction. Man is separate from God but made in his image. He has superiority in creation, above the animals, shown in his capacity to grow close to God. The fundamental thing here is to see the creation of Adam as the beginning of a process in which God gradually forms humanity into what he wants it to be. The stages of life are then a process of growth from innocence to complete humanity. By the end of time, creation and humanity will have grown to their fullness and everything will be as God originally intended it to be. Born in the image but smeared through sin we are on a journey of growing ever more and more closely into God's likeness.

Bible Study Passages

Gen 1:26–31

Gen 3:1–24

2 Pet 1:3–11

Questions for Discussion

In what ways is God a "creator"?

What, for you, is the "image" of God in human beings?

Is there a difference between "image" and "likeness"?

How do you understand the "fall"?

What does it mean for human beings to be "partakers" in God's nature?

Further Reading

Kilner, John F. *Dignity and Destiny: Humanity in the Image of God.* Grand Rapids: Eerdmans, 2015.

Middleton, J. Richard. *The Liberating Image: The Imago Dei in Genesis 1.* Grand Rapids: Brazos, 2005.

DESERT: THE SOUND OF SHEER SILENCE

Advent begins in the desert: in solitude and waiting, in watching and wondering, and in letting go and stripping bare. The desert is something to be embraced and to let happen. Physically, the desert is a place of peace and silence, a place where props and supports disappear, and where boundaries break. The desert is where we are exposed to the stark landscape and the frightening elements. It is where we are dependent and in need. The desert is a place where everything seems to fall away, leaving us engulfed in silence and smallness.

And yet in all this there emerges the deepest experience of the silence of God, the deepest sense of the life of God, and the deepest sense of the reality of faith. For the birth of faith or trust in God takes place in silence: when we are stripped bare of dependency and cover. It takes place when familiar surroundings are removed and comfort zones are left behind. In the abandoned or "deserted" places where we become empty, we meet God, the God of Abraham, Isaac, and Jacob, the God of the prophets of ancient Israel, the God of Jesus and of Muhammad. There in silence we meet the God of the desert, known to so many who have stopped in silence and solitude to listen.

But where is the desert? It has two focal interfacing locations: the physical and the spiritual. The physical landscape is literally the "desert," a particular desert on the earth's surface. The spiritual desert is the inner landscape of the soul or the spirit. First, the physical. It is difficult to define "desert" and there are different sorts. About a third of the earth's surface is desert. Typically, we think of miles of emptiness, the sand dunes in the film *Lawrence of Arabia*.[6] We have probably seen pictures of the Sahara Desert in Africa or the Gobi Desert in Asia. We think of huge uninhabited space with little vegetation or agriculture. We also probably think of intense heat and high temperatures. There's probably little of anything we're used to in the desert: little growth, not much in the way of flora and fauna, it's probably flat though possibly hilly, and it's arid and barren. The desert is empty, harsh, and even hostile. All these characteristics differ in different deserts. The defining feature might be rainfall, or lack of it: a desert usually has less than ten inches of rain a year. The physical desert can be all of these things, but it's usually also a place where we encounter silence, feel exposed, and stripped bare.

And it is precisely here that we connect with the spiritual desert, our own personal inner landscapes of emptiness and silence. In the physical desert and in our own spiritual deserts we feel alone, silent, dependent, out of our comfort zones, and without the usual supports and props. Boundaries disappear and we feel exposed, unsure, and unsafe. The inner spiritual desert of silence, emptiness, and barrenness can take place anywhere. We might suffer from the experience of little growth or life, of losing support or comfort. Our lives might feel broken and stale. We might feel disappointment and anger, regret and loss of hope, little faith in God or human beings. We might feel empty and bored with no sense of creativity or urge for life. And at the point of emptiness and solitude, of barrenness and dependence, the advent of God begins. When we enter the silence and feel stripped bare, the coming of God dawns. And there when we feel empty, we can hear the voice of one who calls us to himself and fills the deepest parts of our longing with a vision of his love.

Paradoxically, this personal, spiritual desert is not unfamiliar to Westerners for whom every physical thing is often provided. And it has been familiar to others too, all over the world, whose inner landscapes have looked dark and dismal. It is not surprising that physical deserts have been metaphors for inner deserts. Outer landscapes have been images for inner landscapes. Indeed, there's a rich literature connecting the two.

---

6. See the film directed by Lean, *Lawrence of Arabia*.

The biblical story takes shape in the desert. The biblical deserts are all different but they each form the context of an important "breaking in" of God. The deserts of Sinai, the Negev, and Judea all have their stories to tell. Abraham is called out from his home in Ur of the Chaldees across the desert in faith and hope, giving up everything he has known, embracing the unknown and encountering God (Gen 12:1–9). The saga of Moses and the formation of the people of Israel is played out in the desert (e.g., Exod 3:1–15; 19:1—20:21; 33:1–23). Later, the prophet Elijah rushes from the complexity of his life and ministry in Samaria down through the Negev to the mountain of Sinai where he encounters God in "a sound of sheer silence" (1 Kgs 19:12).[7] John the Baptist is essentially a desert figure whose ministry is played out in the Judaean wilderness region of the Jordan Valley (Mark 1:4). And Jesus himself is baptized by John and spends time in the desert being tempted by Satan (Matt 3:13—4:11; Mark 1:9–13; Luke 3:21–22 and 4:1–13). All of these biblical, prophetic figures are called out of themselves and stripped bare as they encounter God's presence in the silence of the desert.

Advent begins in the desert. God's coming begins in places of desolation. Look for a place of solitude, of silence, and of peace. Look for a place of dependency on God. Confront your need of him through "letting go" comfort zones that prop you up. Allow some boundaries in your life to be broken and seek what is different. And there at that moment of silent loss and stripping bare, the God of Advent comes to you. Clear the way and make a path for him (Mark 1:3). Hear his call and allow him to embrace you. Your barrenness can then give birth to hope and new life. Ultimately, the desert experience finds an oasis—and God breaks in.

Bible Study Passages

Gen 12:1–9

1 Kgs 19:1–18

Matt 4:1–11

---

7. So, the NRSV. KJV and RSV have the well-known "a still small voice," while the NEB has "a low murmuring sound."

PART 1: THROUGH THE CHURCH'S YEAR

Questions for Discussion

What do you think of when the "desert" is mentioned?

What is a "spiritual desert"?

Relate a time when you have had a "desert experience."

Why is it that God comes to us at times when we are stripped bare?

What was Jesus' experience in the desert?

Further Reading

Lane, Belden C. *The Solace of Fierce Landscapes: Exploring Desert and Mountain Spirituality*. New York: Oxford University Press, 1998.

Ryrie, Alexander. *The Desert Movement: Fresh Perspectives on the Spirituality of the Desert*. Norwich: Canterbury, 2011.

JUSTICE: THE COLOR PURPLE

The color purple is the liturgical color of Advent (and Lent). It is somber and reflective, inviting us to consider more seriously what is approaching at Christmas (and Easter). *The Color Purple* is a novel by Alice Walker that will help us consider what sort of a God it is who comes to us in these purple seasons. Written in 1982, *The Color Purple* has been made into a film by Steven Spielberg and a musical by Russell, Willis, and Bray. Book, film, and musical have all been deservedly popular.

The story of *The Color Purple* is set in Georgia in the American South in the 1930s in a context of racism, oppression, poverty, sexism, and violence. The main character, a young girl called Celie, grows up in a society riddled with every type of injustice. She is abused by her father and has given birth to his child. She also has the child of another man and is then forced to marry yet another man called "mister." Throughout the book there's violence and people in and out of jail. Celie grows up trying desperately to sort out her own identity and who to trust as well as trying to make sense of her faith in God. The novel is written as a series of "letters to God" in which Celie expresses her emotions. Inevitably, she gets angry with what is happening in her life. She also gets angry with God.

Then, Celie's life and sense of God start to change through a religious awakening. Gradually, she starts to see the world differently, noticing small things and connecting them with God. She says she's been trying to get the white man (God) out of her head and then notices something as simple as the color purple. From then on, she sees that all things are connected. She starts to see the deep connection between what God has made and the way people should treat each other. She begins to see the relation between what God is like and what he wants, between the nature of God and how he wants human beings to behave, between God and justice. It's a connection that's all too often missed.

Advent is a good time to read *The Color Purple* and to reflect on the theme of God coming to us in justice. In the Old Testament, justice is part of God's nature and character. He's a just God who wants justice for his people. Justice is essentially what he is like, what he wants, and what he does. He carries out justice and wants to see it realized in creation and society. He wills justice in the relations between his people. And justice has to do, primarily, with people's rights in their communities, not with revenge or getting your own back. God wills to bring fullness, completion, and wholeness as he restores things to a harmonious state. Justice is concerned with the rights of people, with equality, fair distribution of goods, and the care of strangers, orphans, and widows. It's about removing oppression and poverty.

The connection between God's nature and what God wants in terms of justice in society can be seen very clearly in the prophets of ancient Israel. The passages in Amos and Micah are famous: "But let justice roll down like waters," says Amos, "and righteousness like an ever-flowing stream" (5:24). Amos criticizes the rich as they lie on couches drinking wine but have no concern for the poor (6:4–6). Micah complains about similar injustices when he says, "Alas for those who devise wickedness and evil deeds on their beds!" (2:1) and criticizes those who cry peace when there is no justice (3:5–8). The Year of Jubilee in Leviticus 25 is another example of God's concern with justice: every fifty years, land is left fallow to prepare for new growth, and all debts are canceled. It is a leveling of social inequality.

The theme continues in the New Testament. Jesus is portrayed as one who is concerned about the marginalized and the outcast (Mark 5:1–20). He's on the side of those who lack basic needs and is frequently concerned with equality and fairness (Luke 7:36–50). If Matthew 5:6 were translated "Blessed are those who hunger and thirst for justice" (instead of "righteousness"), the meaning would be clearer. St. Paul makes a collection for the poor and needy Christians in Jerusalem (1 Cor 16:1–4) and it is he who makes it clear that God himself gives up his own richness and becomes poor for those he loves (2 Cor 8:9). In all these examples, God's nature is played out in his actions; he wants to see fair and just living among his people. God and justice are intimately connected, and God is known precisely when and where justice is done.

During Advent, Alice Walker's *The Color Purple* can draw our attention to God coming to us in justice. Through the main character, Celie, we are encouraged to look at the small things in life, to see the beauty of creation in a simple color and to make the connections between God's character as it is revealed in creation and the way he wills wholeness and harmony among his people. This is a special way in which God comes to us: as we do his will and partake of his character so we become more familiar with him. There are many, many ways in which our society is riddled with injustice. Like the society that Celie found herself in, we see poverty, sexism, racism, oppression, and violence. But wherever we work to relieve this, God's presence breaks through. As in the Bible, justice isn't getting back at your enemy. It's the establishment of dignity, wholeness, and harmony for all people.

When we see the color purple in church in Advent (and Lent), we're reminded that God wants justice among people and that his very presence breaks through precisely where justice is established.

Bible Study Passages

Amos 5:14–24

Mic 3:1–12

2 Cor 8:8–15

Questions for Discussion

What are your impressions of Celie's ordeal in *The Color Purple*?

What connections do you see between Celie's experiences and life in your own community?

How would you define "justice" and "injustice"?

Why are the Old Testament prophets so concerned about justice?

What can Christians do to establish justice today?

Further Reading

Houston, Walter J. *Justice: The Biblical Challenge*. Oxford: Routledge, 2014.

Walker, Alice. *The Color Purple*. London: W&N, 2017.

MESSENGERS FROM GOD: BE AN ANGEL!

If you drive along the A1 in the north of England or take the train along the East Coast main line, you'll sooner or later see the Angel of the North, the huge statue by Antony Gormley. It stands like a giant dominating the area at Gateshead (Tyne and Wear) and can be seen from miles around. The Angel is an interesting appearance in a secular age like ours. The fact that it's there at all is significant but its size is staggering. Made of steel, it stands 66 feet high with a wingspan of 177 feet. The central body weighs 100 tons and the wings 50 tons apiece. They lean forward slightly, indicating a kind of embrace which gives this steely angel some personality. Set in concrete, the angel can withstand winds of up to 100 mph. Finished in 1998 it cost a million pounds and has largely been accepted into the national imagination. Surely everyone in the UK has at least heard of the Angel of the North and he is famous further afield, too.

It's interesting to speculate on the presence of such a creature dominating the local landscape. Of course, artists and sculptors can choose whatever subject matter they like. There's certainly been a strong interest in angels in recent years, and coffee table books picturing them in art across the centuries have long populated bookshops. But what are angels about and what do they tell us? What lessons can be learned from them? For many people they're ethereal, winged creatures that are difficult to believe in. For others they're very real and some even claim a "guardian angel" is watching over them. In Judaism and Christianity, beginning in the Bible, angels are visitors from the spiritual world. They're "messengers from God."

In the Hebrew Bible there's more than one word for "angel" and different sorts of beings are envisaged when any one word is used. But from the various words and types it's clear that angels are basically "messengers from God." The "angel" (actually a Greek word, *angelos*) communicates with the world on God's behalf. On some occasions, angels appear in a heavenly court or council (Isa 6:1–13; Dan 4:13; 8:13), on others their feet are firmly on earth (Mal 2:7), and on others they seem to be somewhere in between (Gen 18:1–15). Basically, they're mediators between this world and the divine world. In the Second Temple period in Judaism (536 BCE–70 CE) they grew into much greater prominence than before, and their roles expanded. By this time, they were also helpers and protectors as in the famous story of Tobit who has an angel traveling with him on his journey although he doesn't know it! (Tob 5:4; 12:1–22). Sometimes angels are connected with God's activity in creation (Ps 148:1–5), and archangels such as Michael stave off the forces of evil (Dan 12:1–4; Rev 12:7). In general, whenever angels appear, they signify that God is close.

In the New Testament it's much the same. Angels are a sign that God is near. In Luke's gospel, the Angel Gabriel appears to Mary announcing the message from God about Jesus' birth (1:26). In Matthew an angel appears to Joseph to do the same (1:20). Angels also appear when Jesus is born in Bethlehem (Luke 2:8–14), when he is tempted by the devil (Mark 1:13), when he is weak and struggling in Gethsemane (Luke 22:43), at his arrest by the authorities in Jerusalem (at least potentially: Matt 26:53), and at the resurrection (John 20:12) and the ascension (Acts 1:10). St. Paul considered the Jewish law to be given by angels (Gal 3:19; cf. Heb 2:2). The writer of the Letter to the Hebrews clearly knows that angels are important even though Jesus is more so (1:1–14). In the Acts of the Apostles it's an angel that speaks to Moses from the burning bush (7:30) and to Philip on his way to Gaza (8:26). And finally, in the book of Revelation angels are everywhere in the vision of heaven (7:1–3; 8:1–13; 10:1–10). In the New Testament as in the Old, therefore, angels signify God's presence.

Most people think of angels as heavenly creatures with wings. It's a popular image brought to us by Byzantine and Renaissance art and then hardwired into our imaginations. There are famous depictions of angels with wings in art galleries, churches, and cathedrals. They appear as statues and in stunning frescos, icons, and mosaics all over the Christian world. Paintings of the annunciation showing the Angel Gabriel and Mary are among the most famous, and then there are depictions of Jesus' birth and resurrection with angels nearby. The huge Angel of the North fits well into the stereotype we've come to expect: angels are winged messengers, although this one is well over size!

So, what are we to make of these heavenly creatures? They're always cropping up in Bible readings in church. A lot of time and energy can be spent discussing whether or not they really exist and whether we're supposed to think of them as actual creatures in a heavenly realm or just images in literature and art. Either way, it's more important and more challenging to ask what their overall significance is. Surely, it's that we ourselves can be like them. We too can be "messengers from God." Like the many saints in the Christian tradition, angels can be a powerful example to us. They're creatures who reflect the presence of God, bring a message from God or make God's will known to us. They comfort people and give strength and support in difficult times. We too can do these things. We too can be messengers from God, channels of God's grace, offering strength and comfort. We too can take part in God's creativity and even help stave off evil. In the end, wherever we encounter angels, whether it's the giant Angel of the North or any other angel, we are challenged to be like them. They remind us that as Christians we have a serious responsibility and opportunity before us: we can all be angels if we want to be!

Bible Study Passages

Gen 18:1–15

Luke 1:26–38

Rev 12:7–12

Questions for Discussion

What are your impressions of the Angel of the North?

How would you describe an angel?

Have you ever experienced angels?

Do you have a guardian angel and who is it?

In what ways can Christians "be angels"?

Further Reading

Jones, David Albert. *Angels: A Very Short Introduction*. Oxford: Oxford University Press, 2011.

Williams, Jane. *Angels*. Oxford: Lion, 2006.

2

Christmas and Epiphany

BETHLEHEM: THE STOOPING OF GOD

IF YOU GO TO Bethlehem in the Holy Land and stand outside the Church of the Nativity looking at the main doorway, you'll soon notice something rather unusual. The main entrance to the church that stands over the birthplace of Jesus is extremely low and you have to stoop to get in. Once upon a time, in the days of the emperors Constantine and Justinian the main entrance to this church was very grand indeed. The sixth-century Byzantine entrance consisted of three huge doors alongside each other. In the twelfth century, the Crusaders had a lower door. Then in the Ottoman period (1517–1917) the door was lowered even more, so that today the main entrance to one of Christianity's most important shrines is really small: anyone who wants to pass through this door needs to stoop to enter.

The explanation for this low doorway is that animals needed to be kept out and this was the easiest way of doing it. It also kept out unwanted human beings! But the theological explanation is much more interesting: just as God "stooped" in the birth of Jesus to become a human being like us, so we too must stoop to enter the building that marks his birth. For this reason, the door into the Church of the Nativity in Bethlehem is often called the "door of humility": it reflects God's own "stooping" in Jesus.

Christianity could be said to be all about the "stooping of God" and not only in the birth of Jesus although that is the main focus. The first focus of the "stooping of God" is in creation. The idea that God is creator of the world is central to Christianity. He is creator in the book of Genesis (chs. 1–2) and Christians proclaim this regularly when they recite the creed: "We believe in one God, the Father, the Almighty, maker of heaven and earth."[1] When God creates the world, including animals and human beings, he goes out of himself and gives of himself. This is a "stooping" in the sense that he puts himself into what he creates.

The expression "stooping down" is a spatial metaphor capturing the self-giving of God as he gets involved with the world. And of course, God leaves his image on creation as he creates and becomes involved with it. In this sense the notion of God as creator is connected to the experience of God's presence in the world: he has stooped into it. It is often forgotten that in the Prologue to St. John's gospel when it is claimed that "the Word became flesh" in Jesus (John 1:14), this is not the first coming of God into the world. That first stooping is in the creation of the world: "All things came into being through him, and without him not one thing came into being" (1:3). The incarnation of God in Jesus is then the second coming of God into creation, a second "stooping." In this way, creation and incarnation are fundamentally linked together: they are both part of God's stooping to earth.

In his Letter to the Philippians, in the famous "Hymn to Christ" (2:6–11), Paul refers to Christ being "in the form of God" but not needing to cling on to that. Instead, Christ "emptied himself." The Greek word is *kenosis* and has given rise to the expression "kenotic Christology," that is an interpretation of Christ focusing on the idea of him emptying himself of his divinity in the incarnation. This idea is essentially that God "stooped down" in humility in the incarnation and took humanity to himself. Paul says Christ took "the form of a slave" and became like human beings (2:7). This, then, is the human life of Christ in which he serves like a servant and is obedient unto death by crucifixion. The next phase in the stooping process in Philippians is the lifting up: "Therefore God also highly exalted him . . ." Christ is raised up to a position seemingly higher than before and given the most exalted name and lordship—all to God's glory. The threefold pattern of stooping here in Philippians runs like this: Christ is originally in the form of God; he is then humbled unto death; and finally exalted or raised. God's stooping is God's method of exalting.

The theology of John's Prologue and of Philippians is perhaps summed up by Paul's words in his Second Letter to the Corinthians. He says of God, "Though he was rich, yet for your sakes he became poor, so that by his poverty you might become rich" (2 Cor 8:9; cf. 2 Pet 1:4). This entire paradigm of God's stooping action is taken up as a major theme by the fathers of the

---

1. See, e.g., the Church of England's *Common Worship*, 173.

church when they emphasize the incarnation in Christ and its purpose. It can be found in numerous places but Athanasius has the most famous version: "For He became Man that we might be made God."[2] The purpose of God's stooping in Christ is to lift humanity up. The purpose of God becoming human is to take us back with him. And the purpose of God's servanthood is to take humanity into his own life and raise it up. In creation God stoops to create us and in incarnation he stoops to become like us so that we can become more like him.

It is this message of God "stooping" toward us in creation and in Jesus that lies at the heart of the Christian faith and is captured in the surprisingly low door at the Church of the Nativity in Bethlehem. The message of God's stooping is especially important at Christmastime but it is, of course, of the essence of our faith at all times. God goes out of himself in self-giving when he creates the world. The Logos becomes flesh and takes human form. God comes to us in humility and invites us into his own life with him. The little "door of humility" in Bethlehem is really quite appropriate after all: it's about God stooping to come among us.

Bible Study Passages

Gen 1:1–31

John 1:1–18

Phil 2:6–11

Questions for Discussion

What do you understand by the idea of God "stooping"?

What is the relation between God and the world?

What is the meaning of "the Word became flesh"?

Where have you experienced God coming in humility?

How can Christians imitate God's stooping today?

Further Reading

Dennis, Trevor. *The Christmas Stories*. London: SPCK, 2007.

Wright, Tom. *Philippians*. London: SPCK, 2010.

2. See Bindley, *De Incarnatione*, 153.

IN A MANGER: THE CHRISTMAS CRIB

In lots of churches around the world during the Christmas season you'll see cribs or *creches* depicting the birth of Jesus. Mostly, Mary and Joseph stand behind the baby Jesus lying in a manger. There's usually plenty of hay with angels and shepherds standing by. You will almost certainly see sheep, as well, and an ox and ass. A star often hovers overhead reminding viewers of the star that guided the wise men. And by the feast of the Epiphany on January 6 the three wise men themselves will have appeared with their gifts for the child. Other animals might also be present. The crib and figures vary a great deal in size: some are life size, taking up huge amounts of space, while others are tiny. For centuries, churches have had cribs to provide a visual focus of devotion and prayer. Their overall purpose is to remind viewers of the birth of Christ and its significance. As you look into the crib, you yourself become part of the story of the birth of Jesus.

It is usually thought that St. Francis of Assisi invented the Christmas crib following his visit to the Holy Land in 1219. The story is well known: Francis was in Greccio in Italy in 1223 and in order to bring the message of the real humanity of Christ to people he had a real live crib scene during a midnight mass. There were real people, real animals, and a small boy asleep in the manger. From that time onward, it is said, churches began having cribs and later in the seventeenth century people also had them in their homes. In fact, there had already been a devotion to the manger of Jesus by the fifth century. It is claimed that the manger from Bethlehem was in the Church of Santa Maria Maggiore in Rome where it can still be viewed today. In any case, Francis popularized the crib and it is now a familiar part of the Christmas landscape.

What is the message of the Christmas crib? It is surely the same as the message of the gospels themselves: that God came in Jesus and that he is there for all people. Among the gospels, the birth of Jesus is found in Matthew 1 and 2, and Luke 1 and 2. In Matthew, following a genealogy (1:1–17), Joseph receives the message through a dream that Mary his betrothed will give birth to a son (1:18–25). Matthew uses a quotation from Isaiah 7:14 to bring out the relevance of Jesus' birth: "'Look, the virgin shall conceive and bear a son, and they shall name him Emmanuel,' which means, 'God is with us'" (v. 23). The wider significance of the child is then made clear when the wise men from the east appear (2:1–12). They are magi or magicians, probably astrologers. They signify the Gentile world and so point to Jesus' significance beyond Judaism to the outside world. The twofold message is

Part 1: Through the Church's Year

there: Jesus brings God into our midst and he is available to everyone. And even though Matthew's gospel has a predominantly Jewish perspective, it is clear that ultimately Jesus' significance is for all nations (cf. 28:16-20).

In the Gospel of Luke, the story is very different and yet these major themes are there. Luke's story focuses on Mary first. Following the birth of John the Baptist (1:5-25), the annunciation of Jesus' birth comes to Mary through the Angel Gabriel in Nazareth (1:26-38). She is told by the angel that she has found favor with God, that the Holy Spirit will overshadow her, and that Jesus will be the Son of God (v. 35). When Mary and Joseph go to Bethlehem for the census and Jesus' birth (2:1-20) it is clear that Jesus is the savior sent from God (v. 11). In Luke 2:29-32 the prophet Simeon utters what we now know as the Nunc Dimittis ("Master, now you are dismissing your servant in peace") and we are told that Jesus is "a light for revelation to the Gentiles" (v. 32). The double theme is there again: Jesus is from God and brings God to the wider Gentile world. This theme is developed throughout Luke's gospel as Jesus delivers his message beyond the Jewish world to the Gentiles (cf. 8:26-39).

This double theme is also clear in St. John's gospel (1:1-18). Although there is no birth story and no crib scene as such, John's message of God's presence in Jesus is the most powerful in the New Testament. The Logos, the driving rational principle within God himself, takes on flesh and is made known in humility in a human life. "And the Word became flesh" (1:14) turns out to have significance far beyond the Jewish nation: it includes those in darkness such as Nicodemus (3:1-21) but also outsiders such as the Samaritan woman (4:1-42).

The Gospels of Matthew, Luke, and John have different emphases in telling the story of Jesus' birth (Mark says nothing about it). But the twofold message is there in them all: that Jesus comes from God and brings God to a wider people than just the Jews. The same message is captured in the Christmas cribs and *creches* of our churches and homes. The theme of God incarnate in Jesus is there in the presence of the baby. His wider significance is there in the many different characters that are often present in cribs: shepherds, workers, musicians, and passersby, and the many different animals that often appear too. It is also there in the invitation to us to become part of the story and message of the crib.

The practice of having a Christmas creche in churches and homes, whatever the size and detail, is one that should be greatly treasured. Far from being simply a seasonal decoration, it is, as St. Francis intended, a physical depiction of the message of the incarnation and its significance. The crib is a dramatic icon of the message of Christmas and a physical symbol of the deepest dimension of the season: God comes in Jesus and his message and presence are for everyone.

Bible Study Passages

Isa 7:10–17

Matt 1:18–25

Luke 2:8–20

Questions for Discussion

Compare and contrast Matthew and Luke's stories of the birth of Jesus.

Describe some Christmas cribs you have seen.

Does your church have a crib and why?

What is the main message of the crib?

Discuss the significance of the wise men.

Further Reading

Gooder, Paula. *Journey to the Manger: Exploring the Birth of Jesus.* Norwich: Canterbury, 2015.

Kelly, Joseph F. *The Origins of Christmas.* Collegeville: Liturgical, 2004.

MESSIAH: JESUS' GODLY LIFE

Every Christmas, Handel's *Messiah* is performed in towns and cities across the Western world.[3] It's the Christmas music that establishes the season and reinforces an element of religious sentiment even in a secular age. Handel wrote this oratorio in September-October 1741 in just over three weeks using texts from the KJV of the Bible and the Church of England Prayer Book, selected by a wealthy landowner called Charles Jennens. Handel lived in London from 1712 onward, although *Messiah* was first performed in Dublin on April 13, 1742, following an invitation to Handel from the Duke

---

3. A good recording is Parrott, *Handel: Messiah.*

of Devonshire. It was performed for the first time in London the following year. The work was revised numerous times (including once by Mozart) and the original manuscript is now in the British Library in London. Handel's *Messiah* is one of the most famous pieces of music of all time. What's it all about and what does it mean to call Jesus the "messiah" anyway?

The oratorio falls into three parts: part 1 uses prophecies from the book of Isaiah and other Old Testament texts foretelling the birth of Christ, and then moves on to the Annunciation to the Shepherds; part 2 moves through the Passion of Christ to the famous "Hallelujah Chorus," during which King George II allegedly stood up and started a tradition that continues until today; part 3 includes Judgment, the Resurrection of the Dead, and the Glorification of Christ. Made up of recitatives, arias, and choruses, the *Messiah* traces the story of Christ from prophecy to the end of time. But what are we to make of the idea of Jesus as the "messiah" and what is the real focus of the Christmas message of Jesus the messiah?

Messiah is a loaded word in the Bible with very rich backgrounds of meaning in Jewish and Greek thinking and usage. In the Old Testament, the Hebrew word *mashiach* means "anointed one" and is used of a variety of different people. It refers to those who have been especially appointed by God for a specific role. And the ceremony for appointing them is that they get olive oil poured over their heads. *Mashiach* or anointing has to do fundamentally with pouring oil over the head in order to symbolize the appointment. There are three categories of people who get anointed in the Old Testament. First, prophets: for example, Elisha is anointed to follow on the work of Elijah (1 Kgs 19:16). Second, priests: for example, Aaron (Exod 29:7; Lev 8:12) and Zadok (1 Chr 29:22). And third, kings: for example, Saul (1 Sam 9:15–16), David (2 Sam 2:1–7), and Solomon (1 Kgs 1:32–40). These people are God's special agents or instruments, bringing about his will in society and in history. Obviously because they do God's will, they are very closely related to God and his purposes.

It's not surprising, then, that when the early Jewish Christians wanted to say that Jesus was doing God's will, bringing about God's purposes, and acting for God, they used language that they already knew from Judaism. So, it was natural that they should use the word *mashiach*. Jesus was God's messiah or anointed one with a special place in God's purposes. When *mashiach* got translated into Greek, it was natural to look for a word that had to do with "pouring," that is of the oil over the head of the anointed one.

Christmas and Epiphany

This is what the Greek word *christos* means and so it became the translation of *mashiach*. In English this becomes "Christ" or "Messiah."

St. Paul, writing early on in the middle of the first century, uses the word C*hristos* of Jesus about two hundred and fifty times (e.g., Rom 5:6, 8; 1 Cor 8:11; 2 Cor 5:16–20; 1 Thess 5:9). For Paul, Jesus' anointed status clearly involves his death and resurrection but he also uses the word *Christos* as if it's a surname for Jesus: "Jesus Christ." In the gospels the word is there already at the beginning of Mark: "The beginning of the good news of Jesus Christ . . ." (1:1). And probably the most significant occurrence is the answer to the famous question Jesus puts to his disciples near Caesarea Philippi: "Who do people say that I am?" Peter replies, "You are the Messiah" (Mark 8:27–30; Matt 16:13–20). In many cases it sounds like "Christ" really is Jesus' surname but this is far from the truth. The German-American theologian Paul Tillich in his *Systematic Theology* suggests that it would be better to say "Jesus the Christ" or "Jesus who is the Christ" to remind us that "Christ" isn't a surname but a title pointing to who Jesus is: the anointed one of God.[4] And it's important to add that the early Christians saw Jesus as the anointed one of God because of the sort of life he lived, because of his humility and compassion, and because of his death and resurrection. They called him Messiah because they saw God revealed in him. He was Messiah because, like the prophets and many others before him, he did God's will.

When you hear Handel's *Messiah* at Christmastime it's helpful to remember what "messiah" means and why we should take it seriously. The music will surely pull you into a sense of great beauty, and performances will inspire faith and belief. But the central claim that Jesus is the "anointed one" of God is a statement over and over again that he himself did God's will by living a life of compassion and love. A performance of the *Messiah* should inspire us beyond faith and belief into a lifestyle based on Jesus' own lifestyle, a lifestyle that looks like his, and a lifestyle that reflects the life and nature of God himself. Long may the *Messiah* be performed at Christmastime, and long may it inspire not only religious thoughts and warm feelings, but also lifestyles that look like that of Jesus the Messiah himself.

---

4. See Tillich, *Systematic Theology*, 97–98.

PART 1: THROUGH THE CHURCH'S YEAR

Bible Study Passages

2 Sam 2:1–7

Matt 16:13–20

2 Cor 5:16–19

Questions for Discussion

Listen to a section of Handel's *Messiah* and discuss your feelings.

Who were the "anointed ones" of the Old Testament?

Why do God's chosen ones need a special ceremony?

What does "Christ" mean in the New Testament?

In what senses can all Christians be called "Christ"?

Further Reading

Crossan, John Dominic. *Jesus: A Revolutionary Biography*. New York: HarperCollins, 1994.

O'Collins, Gerald. *Christology: A Biblical, Historical, and Systematic Study of Jesus*. Oxford: Oxford University Press, 2009.

EPIPHANY: "SONIC LIGHT"

In recent years, the American musician Morten Lauridsen has become one of the most well-known choral composers of all time.[5] If you've heard his motet *O Magnum Mysterium* (O Great Mystery) you will know why. It was already very well known when it was included in the King's College, Cambridge "Carols from King's" televised in the UK on Christmas Eve 2013. This sent the piece spinning into ever greater popularity and the context added to what is already a most sublime piece of music for voices. The music is for Christmas and takes its text from the service of Matins for Christmas Day. The words express amazement at the sacrament of Jesus' birth from the womb of Mary and that the animals present in the stable should see this event. The music evokes the sheer mystery of the Word made flesh along with its power as a revelation of God. The words fill out the sheer glory and

---

5. For a superb rendition of his significance, see Stillwater, *Shining Night*.

joy of the incarnation of God in Jesus. The piece is enough to bring you to your knees every time you hear it.

Lauridsen is now the most performed American composer of choral music and is playing a big part in the recovery of this type of music in the United States and Europe. He has been professor of music at the University of Southern California, Thornton School of Music since the late 1960s and was given the American National Medal of Arts by the president of the United States in 2007 for his unique contribution to the arts through music. Not only that, Lauridsen is also something of a mystic, which explains a few things about his music. He spends a good part of his time on Waldron Island in the San Juan Archipelago off the northern coast of Washington State in America. A recluse, he lives in the hills looking out across a lake, soaking up the beauty and power of nature. No wonder his music is so deep and wide. He has released over two hundred CDs and has set sacred and secular texts to music, including biblical texts and the poetry of Rainer Maria Rilke and Robert Graves. One of Lauridsen's aims is to produce music which is spiritually transforming and light-giving.

In fact, Lauridsen speaks of his music as light in sound or "sonic light." The music brings light, illumination, radiance, and brightness. It changes the way you see and hear things! It changes perceptions. The music has the mood of timelessness and eternity, of transformation, transfiguration, and new life. It's the music of Christmas, Holy Week, and Easter all rolled into one! Maybe it's the combination of music and poetry that contributes to this as well as Lauridsen's compositional skills. *O Magnum Mysterium* is about Christmas but try listening to it at any time and you will be transformed.

The notion that music might be a kind of shining light, a "musical epiphany," is fascinating. Light is a fundamental image in religion and has played a key part in most religious traditions. At one level it is so basic to human experience that it's not surprising it has been used to try to reflect the reality of God. In Genesis, God creates the light and separates it from the darkness (1:1–5). And in John's gospel, the imagery of light and darkness pervades the Prologue and the rest of the gospel. The darkness doesn't comprehend light (1:4–5). And Jesus himself is the light of the world (8:12). But more important than these examples is the fundamental human experience of God's shining light or brightness in creation and in the experience of God in Jesus and in other places. So, in the Christian traditions of the East, the notion of the "uncreated light" permeates experience, spirituality, and theology. There's the ordinary "created light" of the world and then there's the "uncreated light" which is God himself. The "theology of light" permeates many of the writings of the fathers of the Eastern Church and this is reflected in the theology of icons.

The relevant Old Testament text is the burning bush in which God's shining in creation is imaged in a bush that is on fire but not consumed (Exod 3:1–6). Moses sees God in the bush which symbolizes the whole of creation burning with divine life. This is a form of light shining in creation. The New Testament text that goes with this and is related to it theologically is the transfiguration (Mark 9:2–8). Jesus goes up the mountain and his appearance changes, as does the disciples' perception of him. Jesus' garments are shining white as he is transfigured. The icons of the transfiguration emphasize that this was a moment of divine shining which changed the disciples' entire perception of Jesus and his mission. From then on, everything looked different.

Lauridsen's music, especially the *O Magnum Mysterium*, gives us a "sonic light"—an Epiphany in sound. What the feast of the Epiphany on January 6 celebrates is the shining of God's light in Christ and in the world (Matt 2:1–12). Lauridsen's "sonic light" is a musical version of this same light. The light which the magi see shining in the manger in Bethlehem is God's actual presence spoken of using the metaphor of light. Lauridsen's "sonic light" is a musical naming of God's same shining presence in the world. This is the same light that the biblical texts refer to and which changes our perceptions of everything else when we see it. God breaks through into our lives in numerous places in creation and especially in Jesus. The sense that this presence can take an auditory form moves us a stage further toward understanding that all our senses can be involved in perceiving God. And when we see the light of God in Christ or hear it in music and elsewhere, then other things look and sound different in the light of it. As the psalmist says, "In your light we see light" (Ps 36:9). It is a blinding vision which affects everything else we see.

Bible Study Passages

Gen 1:1–5

Exod 3:1–6

Matt 2:1–12

Questions for Discussion

Listen to Lauridsen's *O Magnum Mysterium* and discuss your reactions.

What is so distinctive about light?

What sense does it make to speak of music as a sort of light?

Where has God's light shone in the world for you?

In what senses is the birth of Jesus a light in the world?

Further Reading

Begbie, Jeremy, ed. *Beholding the Glory: Incarnation through the Arts.* Grand Rapids: Baker, 2001.

Williams, Rowan. *The Dwelling of the Light: Praying with Icons of Christ.* Norwich: Canterbury, 2003.

BAPTISM: REDRAWING THE BOUNDARIES

In the National Gallery in Trafalgar Square in London, among the rich and colorful paintings from between 1250–1500 in the Sainsbury Wing, you can view a very famous work entitled *The Baptism of Christ*, by Piero della Francesca (1415–1492). It's a sizeable canvas (167.5 x 116 cm) worth some serious attention. The scene is familiar to Christians from dozens of other such paintings of this subject and not least from the narratives about Jesus' baptism in the four gospels. The painting and the narratives are layered with symbolism and there's an interesting common thread: boundaries. Christ's baptism marks a boundary between a number of different possibilities and sets new boundaries for those who follow him. It's worth considering Piero della Francesca's painting and then following up parallels in the gospel texts. On the feast of the Baptism of Jesus at the beginning of the new year there's a sobering message about new beginnings for all who are baptized.

Piero della Francesca's *The Baptism of Christ* shows Jesus being baptized by John the Baptist in the River Jordan. The painting (completed around 1460) was originally an altar piece in the Camaldolese Church of Borgo San Sepulchro in Tuscany, Italy, the artist's own town. Indeed, this town is shown in the painting in the distance just below Christ's right arm. The picture shows an arched top with a clear boundary between the sky beyond and the earth below. Christ's body is, of course, central and forms

Part 1: Through the Church's Year

a vertical line including his praying hands, his head, the bowl holding the water and the dove. This line is in parallel with others, forming further boundaries between the angels on the left-hand side, symbolizing stillness and quietness, and the action on the right-hand side, shown in the figure which has either just been baptized or is awaiting baptism. The Pharisees and Sadducees in the background, and John the Baptist himself, all signify a boundary line between the old and the new. Piero's geometric style is also present in the lines and angles formed by John's right arm and left leg. The River Jordan winds its way up to a shallow section in which Jesus is baptized in the forefront of the painting. This also marks a boundary, between the past and what is happening now.

In the gospels, the narrative of Jesus' baptism by John occurs in the three synoptics: Matthew (3:13–17), Mark (1:9–11), and Luke (3:21–22), with only a third-person reference in John's gospel (1:32–34). In all the gospels the baptism is clearly important and marks the beginning of Jesus' ministry. In Mark the account is short but significant elements are there: the River Jordan, baptism by John, the dove, and the opening of heaven. Then the voice announcing to Jesus, "You are my Son, the Beloved; with you I am well pleased." Matthew, also mentioning the Jordan, adds the famous objection by John, "I need to be baptized by you . . ." (3:14), and turns the announcement about Jesus' sonship in Mark into a general announcement, "This is my Son . . ." (v. 17). In a brief reference to the baptism in the second-century *Gospel of the Nazarenes* it is Jesus himself who objects to baptism by John.[6] Luke prunes Matthew and Mark but also adds detail: the Jordan isn't mentioned but there are other people there and Jesus is praying. The dove is now "in bodily form" (v. 22). In the Fourth Gospel there's no baptism narrative as such but John the Baptist says simply that he "saw the Spirit descending from heaven like a dove, and it remained on him" (1:32). Whatever the differences here in these accounts, boundaries have been crossed: heaven has been opened, God has spoken in a new way, Jesus' ministry is inaugurated and a new people are about to be formed.

Perhaps the most striking boundary in the painting and in Matthew and Mark is the River Jordan. This is an allusion that would ring bells for Jews, not only with the crossing of the Red Sea (Exod 13:17—15:27) and thereby the events of the exodus, covenant, torah, and formation of the people of Israel. It would also remind people of the ancient Israelites' own

---

6. For the *Gospel of the Nazarenes*, see Elliott, *Apocryphal New Testament*, 10–14. The reference to Jesus' baptism by John is on p. 13.

crossing of the Jordan into the promised land (Josh 3–5). It was through this very river that the Israelites entered the land and established their new home and identity. It was through this river that the people of God found their new dwelling place, their new home. In the Judaism of Jesus' day there would also have been the act of passing through the water of the *mikveh* or "ritual bath" which was a powerful boundary marker between different parts of Jewish life.

It's a good idea to celebrate the Baptism of the Lord at the beginning of January as a reminder that through his example he leads us forward across boundaries, asking us to go with him into new places. The painting by Piero della Francesca and the gospel narratives all point to the crossing of boundaries of different sorts. For Orthodox Christians, the narratives of the baptism of Christ reveal a thoroughly trinitarian theological emphasis with the Father (the voice), the Son (Jesus), and the Holy Spirit (the dove) all present. Here the very nature of God is revealed as a new stage in history breaks in. At Jesus' baptism, heaven meets earth and he is announced as son of God. The baptism is the initiation of Jesus' forthcoming ministry and way of life. In that life, boundaries are broken and new possibilities emerge.

As in the book of Joshua, Jesus' baptism marks the formation of a particular kind of people who will now follow him and live like him. Here "through the Jordan," boundaries of separation and division (social, economic, and financial; color, gender, and sexuality) are broken down, crossed or redrawn. Followers of Jesus, like Jesus himself, live on the other side of the Jordan. The idea of this river as the image of a new people has been strong throughout history. The feast of the Baptism of Jesus in the River Jordan at the beginning of the new year is a challenging summons to all who follow him: we must cross boundaries and risk new beginnings.

Bible Study Passages

Exod 14:19–31

Josh 3:1–17

Matt 3:13–17

Questions for Discussion

Discuss your reactions to Piero della Francesca's painting.

What are the differences between the gospel accounts of the baptism of Jesus?

What do you understand by "boundaries" in life and in faith?

In what ways does Jesus redraw our boundaries?

In what ways does baptism redefine our lives and values?

Further Reading

McDonnell, Kilian. *The Baptism of Jesus in the Jordan: The Trinitarian and Cosmic Order of Salvation*. Collegeville: Liturgical, 1996.

Wright, Tom. *Mark for Everyone*. London: SPCK, 2001.

3

Lent, Easter, and Ascension

ASH WEDNESDAY: T. S. ELIOT'S JOURNEY

T. S. ELIOT IS ONE of the best known of the twentieth-century English poets and his poem "Ash-Wednesday" is one of his best-known poems. Eliot was actually American. Born in Missouri in 1888 he moved to England in 1914 and took British citizenship in 1927, rejecting his American citizenship. He studied at Harvard in the United States, the Sorbonne in Paris, and at Merton College, Oxford, before moving to London to teach at Birkbeck College. His American-English identity, coupled with the French element, gives his poetry a unique flavor. There is also a personal and spiritual dimension that speaks well beyond the literary world: he is highly respected in religious circles as well.

Eliot's life story forms a significant backdrop to his poetry. He was married twice, first to Vivienne, a marriage that didn't work out, and later to Valerie. His conversion from his native Unitarianism to Anglicanism also played a part. Eliot joined the Anglican Church in 1927 and became churchwarden of St. Stephen's Church, Gloucester Road, London. In England he emerged as a multidimensional figure: poet, playwright, literary critic, and publisher all rolled into one. He was awarded the Nobel Prize for Literature in 1948 and worked for Faber and Faber in London for twenty years. After his death in 1965 his ashes were buried in East Coker in Somerset, the home of his ancestors. He was later included in the famous Poets' Corner in Westminster Abbey in London where a stone in the floor commemorates his life.

Part 1: Through the Church's Year

"Ash-Wednesday" is well known. It was Eliot's first poem after his conversion to the Anglican Church. Published in 1930, it marks his journey from spiritual barrenness to faith. A previous poem, "The Waste Land," traces a similar experience and marks the personal barrenness Eliot experienced during his first marriage. "Ash-Wednesday" captures the author's courage and commitment as he stepped out in a new direction of faith. Based on Dante's *Purgatorio*[1] and evoking something of the purgation experienced during the process, "Ash-Wednesday" captures something of Eliot's struggle in a time of uncertainty and exile.

The poem is divided into six parts each tracking a stage in Eliot's journey. The well-known opening sees Eliot not hoping or expecting to find meaning or fulfilment where he has found them in the past or where most people find them. He doesn't hope to turn again to those same places but expects to rejoice in something new. The movement is away from the appreciation of worldly things to something different. He has, as it were, exceeded his sense of their meaningfulness. Even what seems to be normal and civilized, for example personal ambition, have broken down and become meaningless. Through this experience, Eliot feels tension, exile, and even unworthiness. But it is at the point of despair that newness breaks through. Death gives on to birth. Light breaks into darkness. And revelation comes through barrenness. Eliot has a strong sense of the incarnation of the Word of God breaking through, and it is in the barrenness that faith appears. In all this, prayer is the medium which carries him: "Lord I am not worthy"—"And let my cry come unto thee."

Ash Wednesday, the day in the church's calendar, is the beginning of Lent, one of the most serious seasons of the church's year. It is a season during which there is considerable reflection upon mortality, the meaning of faith, and where we stand before God. Eliot's poem gives us some pointers. On Ash Wednesday we bring before God all our weaknesses and limitations. We bring all our barrenness and sterility in faith. We bring all our doubts and despairs, all our sense of meaninglessness and hopelessness. We bring our experiences of being lost and without direction, of being unfocused or confused, and of being without God. We enter through the wasteland into the beginnings of new possibilities, into a place where God can come to us, and where new life breaks through.

In the Bible there are numerous places where new life breaks through barrenness, sterility, and chaos. For example: the period when ancient Israel

---

1. See Dante, *Divine Comedy*.

was in slavery in Egypt (Exod 1:1—13:16); the period of exile in Babylon when Jerusalem is destroyed and Israel is in a foreign land (Ps 137); the beginning of Jesus' ministry when he is driven into the desert by the Spirit and tempted there (Matt 4:1–11; Mark 1:12–13; Luke 4:1–13); and, of course, the feeling of despair and desertion at Jesus' crucifixion when he cries, "My God, my God, why have you forsaken me?" (Mark 15:34). In all these cases, emptiness and despair eventually break into new life: the people of Israel come out of Egypt and the desert into the promised land (Josh 1–6) and return from exile (the books of Ezra and Neh). Jesus comes out of the desert and begins his ministry (Mark 1:14–15). From abandonment and despair, resurrection bursts forth (Mark 16:1–8).

Eliot's poem "Ash-Wednesday" reflects his own personal story of spiritual wasteland, despair, and conversion. In one form or another, this is the experience of all of us, and surely needs to be. On Ash Wednesday the day, we are all called to the point where we recognize our own despair and move forward into something new, where our own barrenness allows in the light of revelation. Eliot's experience ran along the path of conversion: of life coming out of death, of light shining in darkness, and of the Word of God breaking through despair. Ash Wednesday is the day for us all to begin to confront the emptiness of the way we live, the banality and shallowness of the life our culture and civilization offer us. It is the day to put away greed and personal ambition and to find true depth and meaning in the new life that God offers. It is the day when we can begin to draw back from thinking there is ultimate meaning in the things of this world and refocus our attention on the things of God and the opportunities of a different way of being and living.

Bible Study Passages

Josh 1:1–9

Ps 137

Matt 4:1–11

Questions for Discussion

What are your impressions of Eliot's poem "Ash-Wednesday"?

What is the meaning of the church's season of Lent?

Discuss your own experiences of being in a "wasteland."

Part 1: Through the Church's Year

What was Jesus' experience of loss and despair?

How can new life come out of despair?

Further Reading

Eliot, T. S. "Ash-Wednesday." In *Collected Poems, 1909–1962*. London: Faber and Faber, 1974.

Pritchard, John. *The Journey: With Jesus to Jerusalem and the Cross*. London: SPCK, 2014.

LENT (I): THE INTEGRITY OF JOB

William Blake's paintings are always eerily fascinating.[2] One of my favorite is in the Tate Britain in London and features the Old Testament character Job. It's called *Satan Smiting Job with Sore Boils* and shows Satan standing on Job's body pouring sores all over him from a bottle. Blake worked in the eighteenth and nineteenth centuries and did a lot of Job, including a set of twenty-two engraved prints and two sets of watercolors known after their commissioners as the Butts set and the Linnell set. They cover the whole story of Job. The painting with Satan pouring sores over Job has a particular sting, summing up as it does Job's suffering. Some people think Blake was portraying his own personal suffering in the painting. Of course, it is usually thought that Job's unexplained suffering is the key theme of the book of Job and it is certainly central. But there are other themes in addition to theodicy (the explanation of God's goodness in the face of human suffering). In fact, no answer is ever given as to why Job is suffering; perhaps the real message lies in another aspect of the story.

The proverbial "patience of Job" is an alternative focus: it is Job's patience which is his prime virtue, we are told, and which we should emulate. Indeed, this has been a significant interpretation in the Christian tradition (Jas 5:11).[3] And certainly, Job displays patience but I'm sure there's more even than this in what is the most drawn-out and dramatic saga in the Bible. In the end, it is Job's integrity that is being tested in the story, and

---

2. For an up-to-date assessment of Blake's significance, see the catalogue for the 2019–20 Blake exhibition at the Tate Britain in London, Myrone and Concannon, *William Blake*.

3. At Jas 5:11 the NRSV has "endurance," while the RSV has "steadfastness," and the NEB says that Job "stood firm." The traditional "patience" is from the KJV.

the whole tale revolves around his reaction, sincerity, and motivation. The story of Job might pose the question about God's behavior but it also asks one about Job's integrity.

As is well known, Job is an upright and righteous non-Israelite man from the land of Uz (1:1). He is blameless before God and treats his fellow human beings with care and concern. Nothing seems to stand between Job and God, and indeed Job is blessed many times over, having many sons, daughters, slaves, and cattle. Everything seems to be as it should be for Job: he is healthy, wealthy, and wise and has the respect of everyone around him. He is a fine example of the way things should be (1:1–5).

But God and Satan are in cahoots (1:6–12) and one day a messenger comes to Job and tells him that all his animals, sons, and daughters are dead, following attack by foreigners and natural disaster (1:13–22). Then, Job himself becomes ill with sores and ulcers covering his entire body (2:1–10). In his pain and distress, he sits on a pile of ashes scratching his sores with a piece of broken pottery (2:8). This is the scene captured in Blake's painting. Job loses the respect of all around him, who conclude that he must have sinned if God treats him like this. The notion of divine retribution (that God punishes with suffering those who sin) permeates the whole story and even Job himself, who knows he hasn't sinned, believes his suffering is unjust. Three friends, the famous "Comforters," help Job but they provide little real comfort (2:11–13; 3:1—27:23).

As the story develops and the drama builds, Job wishes he'd never been born (3:11–16; 10:18–22). But he does not curse God or question God's power and majesty in spite of promptings to do so from those around him. Indeed, Job wants to be honest with God. He brings his anger, his emotions, and his feelings of being treated unjustly, all before God. But in trying to test God, Job is being tested himself. His sincerity, motivation, integrity, and faithfulness are all on the line. What were his real motives, and why was he so righteous in the first place? Was he trying to win his way to heaven? Indeed, Job's belief that his suffering is unjust shows him to believe in divine retribution. But God wants Job's faithfulness for its own sake. And Job is faithful: his famous words come at the point of his greatest despair: "For I know that my Redeemer lives" (19:25). And finally, God speaks to Job out of the whirlwind (38:1) not providing answers or explaining himself but showing himself to be a friend who listens to Job whatever he has to say. And in the end, Job comes to know a very different sort of God from the one he was questioning. His integrity has been tested through suffering, pain, and despair and he has proved himself not just patient but faithful (42:1–6).

During Lent, Job could easily be a model for all of us to contemplate. We resonate with his suffering and his cries of injustice. We know what he is going through and how unjustly dealt with he feels. We ourselves question God's behavior and seeming injustice. And we may or may not have patience like Job. But usually we do not get the deeper message of Job's story. We may not realize that in all our questioning of God, it is we ourselves who are being questioned and tested. It is our own integrity that is undergoing scrutiny. It is our motivation, sincerity, and faithfulness that are on the line. And we may not understand that, like Job, through the testing we can come to know a different God from the one we expected, a God who will listen to our anger and our cries of injustice, a God who will be there for us as a friend whenever we need him, but a God who will still test us, nevertheless.

Blake's painting of *Satan Smiting Job with Sore Boils* in the Tate Britain captures a great deal of Job's pain and suffering and probably a good deal of his patience as well. But it also catches that element in the story of Job which challenges all of us to examine our lives before God, our motives for doing religious things, and our integrity in faith. In Lent, or at any time, the story of Job puts us all on the spot.

Bible Study Passages

Job 1:1–22

Job 38:1–11

Jas 5:7–11

Questions for Discussion

If God is good, why do human beings suffer?

What is the relation between good and evil?

Is Job justified in trying to bring God to trial?

What do you make of Job's "patience"?

What sort of God does Job end up knowing?

Further Reading

Goldingay, John. *Job for Everyone*. London: SPCK, 2013.

Jung, Carl Gustav. *Answer to Job*. Oxford: Routledge, 2002.

LENT (II): ABIDING

Look into any realtor's or estate agent's window in any location and you'll see desirable property for sale. Hopefully, if you're looking to buy, some of it might be within reach. Probably, as house prices go, much of it will be well out of reach. If you're looking to buy, the process gets more complicated the more you look. Perhaps you know what you want but can't see it. Perhaps you see what you want but can't afford it.

For most of us, finding the right house is important: it's going to be where we live and where we spend a lot of our time. It's the place we return to after work, the place we work from, perhaps, and hopefully the place where we relax. Homes reflect who we are, our social status, personalities and dreams. When we buy a property, it becomes the place where we "bed down"; we bond with it and make it our own. We not only take up residence in our homes but it feels like they take up residence in us. We soon know if we don't feel comfortable in a house, and we can settle in so much that we find it hard to leave. Our house is our dwelling place, our resting place, and our abode. There's a sense of identity involved.

The Archbishop of Canterbury's Lent Book for 2013 was written by the Professor of Christianity and the Arts at King's College, London: Ben Quash. The title is simply *Abiding*. It is a reflective work looking at the whole idea of "abiding" as it might be understood in Christian theology and life. Each chapter leads the reader through a meditation on why this rather old-fashioned and neglected word is really quite important. Although not widely used these days, to "abide" basically means to "wait," "stay" or "remain" in a location or to "be with" someone. Quash shows how Christians abide in places through their bodies. We inhabit the places we live in, we inhabit churches and communities. Life in a religious community is a good example of abiding bodily in a location. We can also "abide" in things through our minds. Quash encourages us to abide in the texts of the Bible, remaining with them reflectively, inhabiting them, and becoming familiar with them. And we can also inhabit other people in our many different sorts of relationships with them: through caring and in suffering with others. Finally, we "abide" when we are away from our usual dwelling places, when we are at peace in total relaxation, and of course after death when we abide with God. In all these places and ways, Quash shows, we dwell or abide within something.

The key biblical use of the concept of abiding comes in St. John's gospel in the so-called Farewell Discourses of chapters 14–16. The second part of the gospel opens with chapter 13, where Jesus washes his disciples' feet and sets an example for them to follow. Beginning with the Last Supper scene, this is the beginning of the journey to the cross. The sense of the relation between Jesus and God, and between Jesus and the disciples is deepening. Now in chapter 14 the concept of "indwelling" emerges. We are told that Jesus is "in" the Father and the Father is "in" him (14:10–11).

In John 15 this concept of "indwelling" comes specifically in relation to the word "abide" and is now wrapped up in the metaphor of the vine. The vine is a well-known symbol of ancient Israel (see Isa 5:1–7; Mark 12:1–12). In John's gospel, it symbolizes Jesus and the disciples. The branches of a vine dwell or abide in the vine itself. The branch cannot bear fruit unless it abides or dwells in the main part of the vine, so Jesus' disciples will not bear fruit unless they abide or dwell in him. The passage culminates in Jesus saying, "Abide in my love" (v. 9). The concept of abiding comes to a climax in chapter 17 where Jesus speaks about God being in him and he in God (v. 21). Overall, as the plot thickens in the second half of John's gospel, there's a deepening sense of the relationship between Jesus and his Father, a relationship which Jesus hopes the disciples will find too. And the notion of indwelling or abiding in these chapters gives a powerful message for all Christians: we are to dwell "in" God and let God dwell "in" us.

Our homes are important to us. We dwell or abide in them. We make our home in them and find our identity in them. Homes are places from which we go out energized and refreshed and to which we return to find rest and peace. And this notion of abiding, inhabiting, or indwelling is a very powerful "container metaphor" for our relationship with God. Can we live "inside" God and let God live "inside" us? In John 15:1–11, the vine and branches are essentially related, each being "in" the other. Jesus and his disciples have a relation of mutual indwelling and abiding. Through this word and through the vine image we are told that God and Jesus dwell in us and take up residence in us. And we dwell in God and in Jesus. It is no accident that at the beginning of John's gospel we are told that "the Word became flesh and lived among us" (1:14), where the word for "lived" means a tent or dwelling place.

As Christians we do not chase a distant or remote God; we inhabit or abide in God and God dwells and abides in us. We live in God and make God our home (like a swimmer immersed in water) and God lives in us. St. Paul surely knows the same truth when he writes of being "in Christ" and of Christ dwelling "in" us (Rom 8:9–11; 2 Cor 5:17; Gal 2:20). Together, then, God and Christ provide our dwelling place, our identity, and our real home.

Bible Study Passages

John 14:8–11

John 15:1–11

Rom 8:9–11

Questions for Discussion

Share some experiences of living in different houses. What is unique about them?

Where do you feel most "at home"?

What other examples of abiding in something do you know?

Discuss what it means to say that Jesus abides in God.

In what senses do you experience God and Jesus abiding in you?

Further Reading

Inge, John. *A Christian Theology of Place*. Oxford: Routledge, 2016.

Quash, Ben. *Abiding*. London: Bloomsbury, 2012.

LENT (III): THE RICH FOOL

One of my favorite Roald Dahl short stories is "Parson's Pleasure" in a collection called *Kiss Kiss*. It concerns a certain Cyril Boggis, expert antiques dealer and mock clergyman. In order to boost his business, he puts on a dog collar and visits houses in rural areas to see what possible purchases might lie within. He goes to any lengths of deception to pay as little as possible for a piece of the greatest value. Boggis combines his love of antiques with a love of wealth.

One day this deceiver manages to get into a farmhouse in Berkshire, England, and sees the most amazing Chippendale commode worth a possible twenty thousand pounds. The owners know nothing of its real value so Boggis proceeds by reinforcing its worthlessness. It seems they originally paid more than Boggis now offers but through sustained persuasion the bogus clergyman convinces them it's fake. He really isn't interested in it, he tells them, and might just be able to use the legs for something. It's only worth chopping up for firewood, he emphasizes. The owners finally get Boggis to agree to give them twenty pounds to take the commode away. While he has gone up the road to get his car, the deceived farmers decide (now accepting the piece as totally worthless) that the odd clergyman in their midst is unlikely to be able to get the item into his car so they chop it up into small pieces, knowing he won't mind! A classic Roald Dahl twist in the tale hangs over the end of the story as Boggis makes his way back to the house to pick up his prize twenty-thousand-pound commode!

Apart from being a really good read with a gripping style, perfectly controlled sense of suspense, and with the final climax outside the story, there's a strong message in this tale: wealth and greed bring their own rewards. The Bible has something to say about this. The Old Testament is clear that God wants the rich to look after the poor. The prophets of ancient Israel speak out against wealthy people who neglect the poor (e.g., Amos 2:6–8; 4:1; 5:11) and gaining wealth at the expense of others is criticized (e.g., Amos 8:4–6; Mic 2:1–3; Isa 10:1–2). Wealth can be a blessing as well as a curse but it mostly leads in a bad direction (e.g., Prov 3:16; Ezek 7:11). The New Testament also shows a strong bias against wealth and greed (Matt 6:24). The story of the Rich Young Man is a good example (Matt 19:16–22; Mark 10:17–22; Luke 18:18–23). Jesus says it's impossible to enter the kingdom of God if you're rich (Matt 19:23–26; Mark 10:23–31; Luke 18:24–27) and the rich do not go to heaven (Luke 16:19–31). In the Epistle of James, whose focus is on practical faith or ethics, it's clear that the rich get rich at the expense of the poor and that they will face judgment in the end (5:1–12).

One of the most important parables in the gospels about wealth and riches is the Parable of the Rich Fool in Luke 12:16–21. A man's land produces a good crop and he wonders where to store it. He decides to build larger barns and sit back and enjoy it. But God says, "You fool! This very night your life is being demanded of you" (12:20). Among the gospels the story is only in Luke although there's a similar one in the *Gospel of Thomas* (63).[4] The Thomas version is shorter and somewhat more direct: a rich man has money and wants to develop his wealth and store his crops. But that night he dies.

The parable in Luke raises serious questions about wealth and what to do with it, as well as about discipleship, life, and death. It might be said that the man in the parable didn't actually pursue wealth, but his land produces it so he obviously has some interest in it. He then decides to store it up and sit back. In the end, the story is about the man's ultimate values and his desire for material comfort and stability. It's about his treasure on earth and where he puts his trust (cf. Matt 6:21). It's also about the fact that life can be cut short at any moment, and the saying at the end of this story sums that up: God reminds him that his life will end. The man may be rich in worldly terms but he is "not rich toward God" (Luke 12:21). Luke's Parable of the Rich Fool stands in line with his wider interests in the poor and outcast (cf. Luke 1:46–55; 10:25–37).

Luke's Rich Fool and a great deal of the other material in the Bible about wealth resonates with Dahl's mock clergyman in his "Parson's Pleasure" story. It all teaches us that storing up treasure for ourselves on earth doesn't lead to real riches. In Dahl's tale, of course, there's no mention of heaven, but the fact that Cyril Boggis is dressed up as a clergyman brings the theme of religion into the story. Nor are heaven and the afterlife mentioned by Dahl but Boggis's disappointment comes before he even leaves the property of those he is deceiving. He has misled innocent people for his own gain and has ended up losing what he thought he was gaining. In the end, of course, Boggis deceives himself just like the Rich Fool and all those who pursue wealth for its own sake.

For Christians, all this presents a real challenge to faith. The First Epistle to Timothy tells us that "the love of money is a root of all kinds of evil" (6:10) and although money can do wonderful things and there's nothing wrong with using it for good purposes, idolizing it and making it our central quest in life will lead to great disappointment both here on earth and after death. First Timothy continues in similar vein: "In their eagerness to be rich some have wandered away from the faith and pierced themselves with many pains."

---

4. For *The Gospel of Thomas*, see Elliott, *Apocryphal New Testament*, 123–47. The Rich Fool appears on p. 143, para. 63.

PART 1: THROUGH THE CHURCH'S YEAR

Bible Study Passages

Amos 8:1–8

Mark 10:17–22

Luke 12:16–21

Questions for Discussion

What are your reactions to the behavior of Cyril Boggis in Dahl's story?

What does the Bible have to say about wealth?

What is the message of Luke's parable of the Rich Fool?

Discuss good and bad things that result from wealth.

What should Christians do with their wealth?

Further Reading

Dahl, Roald. "Parson's Pleasure." In *Kiss Kiss: Expect the Unexpected*. London: Penguin, 2011.

Witherington, Ben, III. *Jesus and Money*. London: SPCK, 2010.

PALM SUNDAY: JOINING IN THE STORY

In Jerusalem, the "Palm Sunday Church" is a small nineteenth-century building at Bethphage on the Mount of Olives not far from Bethany. Bethphage is the location named in the gospels as the place from which Jesus sent his disciples into the city to get the donkey and from which his "Palm Sunday ride" began (Matt 21:1–11; Mark 11:1–11; Luke 19:28–40; John 12:12–19). In Hebrew, Bethphage means "the house of the young fig" and it has the sense of pointing to the future when there will be growth and ripeness. Every year on Palm Sunday a procession begins from this church, moves across the Kidron Valley, and enters the Old City of Jerusalem, recalling Jesus' own journey and marking the beginning of Holy Week. The little church at Bethphage dates back to 1883 and the original location of the place isn't known although there were Byzantine and Crusader churches there. The modern church is a small Franciscan chapel with a simple altar and frescos around the walls. It's a small but extremely moving place of prayer.

Renovated in the mid-1950s by the well-known Italian architect Antonio Barluzzi, the church has a striking fresco painted by Cesare Vagarini in the apse behind the altar. Not surprisingly it is a depiction of the Palm Sunday ride with Jesus on a donkey and people standing by, laying their garments on the road, and waving palm branches. Presumably they are shouting "Hosanna" or "Lord, save us." But there is a surprising feature in the picture: one of the figures standing by has a sheet over its head. This often raises the curiosity of pilgrims and visitors. Who is the person? Is it one of the disciples or another of the characters in the Palm Sunday story? Or perhaps it's the artist who painted the fresco? The hidden identity sets the imagination running wild. Could the figure even be you, the person looking at the picture? And if so, what are the implications of this?

Working on this interpretation (that the person under the sheet is anyone who looks at the painting) the message is that everyone is invited into Jesus' story. For the hidden identity, we substitute ourselves. We ourselves can be there participating in the Palm Sunday event. We ourselves can lay our garments, wave our palms, and even follow Jesus into the city right through to his final moments, to his death and resurrection. Indeed, interpreted in this way, this painting represents an invitation to us all to enter Jesus' story from the beginning and not just during the last week. This is not just a liturgical invitation to walk the Palm Sunday procession or enter into the last days of Jesus' life in prayer and meditation. The painting effectively invites Christians into Jesus' story from the beginning of his life as we know it from the gospels. It's an invitation to follow him, to become disciples of his. It's an invitation to form and shape our lives on his to such a degree that we become like him. We too, the painting suggests, can have a part in his story.

In recent years there's been a great deal of emphasis on the importance of stories, not just in religion but in almost every branch of learning. Stories are powerful and life-shaping, they are formative and life-giving. The story you follow is your identity and the way you make sense of the world. In religion and theology, stories have been emphasized as the vehicles we use for knowing God and living in relation to him. The world is "story shaped" and stories lead us to truth more effectively than abstract philosophizing and speculation. And it's not just a matter of deciding, for example, which character in a parable from the gospel story we might align ourselves with, or seeing which disciple we are most like. It's a matter of becoming more and more like Jesus himself through following him and staying with him throughout his story.

The gospels tell us early on that Jesus called disciples to follow him (e.g., Mark 1:16–20; 3:13–19). The sense in the texts is that they responded pretty immediately and gave up everything to be with him. They are then alongside him through the many things he undergoes: the ups and downs, the uncertainties, and the challenges. They are the recipients of his teaching about the kingdom of God in parables and miracles, and they are invited at Caesarea Philippi to reaffirm their commitment (Mark 8:27–33). An inner group of disciples develops (Mark 5:37; 9:2; 13:3; 14:33) but they are all there by implication as the journey to the cross gets closer and closer. The disciples are by no means the perfect band of followers; they flounder and are weak, they question, misunderstand, and deny (Mark 6:6, 52; 9:32; 14:66–72). Some stay with Jesus through doubts, misunderstandings, and weaknesses. Some remain with him as their perception deepens and they start to realize what he is really about. Others flee and betray him, unable to make the full course. But in any case, the message is clear: being a disciple involves being part of the story.

The painting in the apse of the little Palm Sunday church at Bethphage on the Mount of Olives in Jerusalem calls Christian disciples to follow Jesus. Not that it will always be straightforward or easy and not that we won't experience failure and weakness. But we can join in the story from wherever we are and play our own part in it. The painting of Jesus' "Palm Sunday ride" into Jerusalem reminds us that we are all invited to join the way of Jesus, to adopt his lifestyle, and to follow him to the end. And that includes being disciples who are willing to learn from his teaching, willing to try to change in the light of his message, and willing to take his life as an example of how to live. Palm Sunday asks us whether or not we can live in Jesus' story, align our identity with his, and grow more and more like him.

Bible Study Passages

Matt 21:1–11

Mark 1:16–20

Mark 14:66–72

Questions for Discussion

What does "joining in the story of Jesus" mean to you?

Name some of Jesus' disciples. What were they like?

What is the message of Jesus' "Palm Sunday ride"?

Discuss times when you have been uncertain about your discipleship.

How does being a disciple of Jesus bring you joy and strength?

Further Reading

Rhoads, David, and Donald Michie. *Mark as Story: An Introduction to the Narrative of a Gospel*. Philadelphia: Fortress, 1982.

Tilley, Terrence W. *Story Theology*. Collegeville: Liturgical, 2002.

THE LAST SUPPER: WHO ARE WE?

If you're ever in Milan, Italy, it's more than well worthwhile getting tickets to see the famous Leonardo da Vinci painting *The Last Supper*. It must be one of the most famous paintings in the world and a visit really does repay all the queueing and waiting. The painting can be found in the refectory at the Church of Santa Maria Della Grazia and dates from the late fifteenth century. Leonardo (1452–1519) was commissioned to do the painting by the then Duke of Milan, Ludovico Sforza, and carried out the work between 1494 and 1498. Not that he worked on it continuously; apparently, he would go in and do a bit now and then!

Last Supper paintings were common in the period of the High Renaissance but Leonardo's is unique and has been the subject of a great deal of controversy and debate by art historians and others. It has had multiple interpretations (one of the latest by Dan Brown in his best-selling novel *The Da Vinci Code*[5]) and numerous renovations. In fact, at times the painting has been in such bad condition that it has been almost repainted in order to help it survive humidity, crumbling, and flaking—and a bomb in 1943. As you file past it, looking at Jesus in the center of the table with six disciples on each side, you sense a feeling of being drawn into a family event and yet of being simultaneously confronted and challenged by it.

---

5. Brown, *Da Vinci Code*.

Part 1: Through the Church's Year

What's going on in the painting takes a bit of time to appreciate as the detail is considerable and it's still in a pretty bad condition. At first sight, the moment depicted in *The Last Supper* seems to be the one in which Jesus is saying, "this is my body" and "this is my blood." "The Last Supper," of course, was Jesus' last meal with his disciples the night before he died. It was most probably a Passover meal, the great annual meal at the celebration of Passover, the Jewish feast of liberation from slavery in Egypt (Exod 12:1–28). The Passover meal took place the night before the feast and symbolized everything that had happened in Egypt. For Jews, it was (and still is) a celebration of liberation from slavery.

In the Synoptic Gospels, Jesus eats this meal with his disciples the night before the crucifixion (Matt 26:26–30; Mark 14:22–26; Luke 22:14–23). The different accounts have different details and different emphases but during the meal Jesus takes bread and wine and says the words "this is my body," "this is my blood" over them, signifying a connection with his coming death the next day.[6] The earliest account of the Last Supper comes in St. Paul's First Letter to the Corinthians where the same connection is made (11:23–26). In Christianity through the centuries, the Last Supper has been the focal event of worship in most churches. For many interpreters of Da Vinci's painting, this is the primary emphasis: it is the institution of the Lord's Supper, Eucharist, Holy Communion or Mass.

But there's more here as well. Some scholars have suggested that the moment depicted in the painting is when Jesus announces that someone will betray him (e.g., Mark 14:18). You can certainly see the disciples' various reactions, their faces, gesticulations, and body language—and what they're probably saying to Jesus and to each other. In the gospels, the lists of Jesus' twelve disciples differ (Matt 10:1–4; Mark 3:13–19; Luke 6:12–16; cf. Acts 1:13) and we learn very little about their characters. Peter and Judas come over in sharper relief (Matt 26:14–16; 27:3–10; Mark 14:53–72;) and maybe even James and John (Mark 10:35–40) but the detail on the others is thin or absent.

However, in this painting Leonardo captures the movement and dynamism of the moment and brings more to the disciples' characters than the gospels do. Here their faces reveal who they are. Shock and horror can be seen, outrage and self-questioning, a sense of confrontation with themselves, suspicion and disbelief, and of course the hope that it's not they who

---

6. In St. John's gospel the occasion focuses on Jesus washing his disciples' feet and there is no bread or wine (13:2–11).

will betray Jesus. In the painting, each disciple plays a part in the unfolding drama; and what better moment for their characters to emerge than during a meal of liberation? What better time for the disciples to be confronted with their own role in the story? What better moment to make the decision of whether and in what sense they are really with him? Some characters are exposed more than others: Peter has a knife, Thomas points to heaven, and Judas, who will betray him, is painted in dark shadow.

Filing past Leonardo's painting in Santa Maria Della Gracia, Milan, is a moment most visitors will never forget. The painting gets imprinted on the minds and souls of most who see it. And for Christians, the experience reaches deeper levels of meaning and significance. We are drawn in but also confronted and challenged. We become part of a family event but our characters are exposed and questioned. Whether we stand before the painting in Milan or come to the Eucharist on Maundy Thursday (or at any other time), the two elements are there. We belong at the meal and are welcome at it but we are challenged as well. What character do we bring and what level of commitment? What is the meaning of the event for us and where do we fit in around the table? What are our reactions to Jesus' announcements of body and blood, and betrayal? And are we able to stay with him or will we desert him in the end?

Da Vinci's painting *The Last Supper* isn't only a masterpiece of Western art. It refocuses the Christian mind on where we fit in at the table, on what our ultimate motives are, and on whether we have the strength, courage, and commitment to stay with Jesus through the coming days of our lives. Both painting and Eucharist are an affirmation and incorporation, and yet a confrontation and a challenge to our very identity as Christians.

Bible Study Passages

Exod 12:1–28

Luke 22:14–23

1 Cor 11:23–32

Questions for Discussion

Discuss the meaning of the Passover meal in Judaism.

What is your understanding of Jesus' last meal with his disciples?

What does St. Paul have to say about the Last Supper?

PART 1: THROUGH THE CHURCH'S YEAR

What is your understanding of the Eucharist?

In what ways does the Eucharist challenge us as Christians?

Further Reading

Ladwein, Michael. *Leonardo Da Vinci, the Last Supper: A Cosmic Drama and an Act of Redemption*. Sussex: Temple Lodge, 2006.

Witherington, Ben, III. *Making a Meal of It: Rethinking the Theology of the Lord's Supper*. Waco: Baylor University Press, 2007.

GOOD FRIDAY (I): THE KELHAM ROOD

Inside the Church of St. John the Divine, Kennington, in South London, there stands a life-size crucifixion scene known as the "Kelham Rood." A "rood" is a crucifix with Jesus' mother standing on one side and the beloved disciple standing on the other as mentioned in St. John's gospel (19:26–27). The "Kelham Rood" comes originally from Kelham Hall in Nottinghamshire where it dominated from a great height the domed chapel of the Church of England Theological College founded in the early twentieth century by the religious community known as the Society of the Sacred Mission (SSM). Sculpted by Charles Sargeant Jagger (1885–1934) the rood left Kelham when the Theological College closed in 1973, and was taken to Willan Priory in Milton Keynes where SSM made its new home. The three figures stood in the garden at Willan for over thirty years until they were restored by Rupert Harris in 2003 and taken to St. John's Church in Kennington in 2004.

The figures of the Kelham Rood are no ordinary statues: their impact is startling and even shocking. The crucified Christ is bound to the cross with ropes. His sturdy figure rises somehow above the human suffering visible in his limbs. The mother of Jesus holds up her hands in desperation while the beloved disciple covers his face in shock and grief. The entire scene speaks of the humanity and suffering of Jesus, of the tragedy of his death, and of the pain experienced by him and those close to him. But it also speaks of what is accomplished in that death and in that pain. This is the death of the one who overcomes despair and death, opening up a new sense of God's ways with the world. This is the Christ of St. John's gospel, whose suffering is also his exaltation.

How are Christians to think of the meaning of the crucifixion of Jesus, especially on Good Friday? What message does the cross give us? After all, it is the dominant symbol of Christian faith and every Christian needs some awareness of what it means. Already in the writings of St. Paul, the crucifixion is central. In 1 Corinthians, he says that the cross is the central message to the Corinthians (2:2), even though the resurrection is also key (15:1–58). And Paul clearly sees weakness and suffering as part of God's ways with the world and with Jesus. Christ is the power of God and the wisdom of God, to be contrasted with worldly power and wisdom, and the "foolishness of God" (or his wisdom) is epitomized in the cross of Jesus (1:20–25).

There is further emphasis on the cross in the gospels and this can be seen especially in the final words of Jesus as he dies. In St. Mark's gospel, the cross casts its shadow from the beginning and the coming suffering of Jesus is a recurring theme throughout (8:31; 9:31; 10:33; 10:45). Jesus' words from the cross in Mark are, "My God, my God, why have you forsaken me?" (15:34). They show the darkness of Jesus feeling abandoned by God. In Matthew's gospel Jesus' final words are the same (27:46) although Matthew has resurrection appearances as well (28:1–20). In Luke, the cross permeates the gospel but the final words of Jesus give a different theological mood: "Father, into your hands I commend my spirit" (23:46). Here Jesus is in charge of what is happening to him, more of a passive figure in God's purposes.

It is, however, in the Gospel of John that a deeper theology of the cross emerges. As in the other gospels the shadow of the cross falls over the whole narrative but now the exaltation of Jesus comes with it. Frequent references to the coming "hour" point forward to Jesus' death. At the wedding at Cana the "hour" has not yet come (2:4); in Jerusalem at the Feast of Tabernacles, the "hour" has still not come (7:30); when Jesus is teaching in the temple the "hour" has still not yet come (8:20). In 12:23 Jesus says, "The hour has come for the Son of Man to be glorified" and when he is teaching about the coming of the Holy Spirit, he indicates that the "hour is coming" (16:25). In the prayer he offers to God before his passion begins, the "hour has come" (17:1). Another indicator of the cross coming in John's gospel are the references to Jesus' being "lifted up." The Son of Man will be "lifted up" like Moses lifted up the serpent in the wilderness (3:14). And in 12:32–33 Jesus says, "And I, when I am lifted up from the earth, will draw all people to myself." The gospel writer adds, "He said this to indicate the kind of death he was to die."

The imagery of the "hour" and the "lifting up" in John's gospel both point to Jesus' crucifixion but carry something much more than the cross alone. Here the crucifixion when it comes is also exaltation; the moment of suffering and death is also the moment of resurrection. Here Jesus' final words from the cross, "It is finished" or "it is accomplished"[7] (19:30), indicate that Jesus' death overcomes all things. The cross is crucifixion and exaltation together. The cross itself is the life-giving moment of resurrection.

A visit to the Kelham Rood in the Church of St. John the Divine, Kennington in London can be a daunting experience. Brooding as they do over prayerful onlookers the figures tell the story of suffering and death, of grief and pain. And yet the figure of Christ somehow rises up above the suffering. The shadow of death and grief is black and yet Jesus' enormous strength and overcoming shine out. Through his pain and suffering, his endurance and power are evident. This is the Johannine Christ triumphing over death and rising as he does so. And there is a message here for all Christians, especially on Good Friday, about the meaning of the glorious cross: death and resurrection are part of the same reality.

Bible Study Passages

Mark 15:33–39

Luke 23:44–49

John 19:28–30

Questions for Discussion

Discuss different depictions you have seen of the crucifixion.

What do the gospels say about Jesus' death on the cross?

How can a death also be life-giving?

What is your experience of new life coming out of grief and despair?

What would your "theology of the cross" look like?

---

7. The New English Bible has this.

Further Reading

Aulén, Gustaf. *Christus Victor: An Historical Study of the Three Main Types of the Idea of the Atonement*. London: SPCK, 2010.

Tomlin, Graham. *Looking Through the Cross*. London: Bloomsbury, 2013.

GOOD FRIDAY (II): *NIGHT*

In 1986, the Romanian-born American Jewish writer and political activist Elie Wiesel won the Nobel Peace Prize for his work for peace and reconciliation. Wiesel was a Holocaust survivor and well-known author and lecturer. One of his books, *Night*, tells of his childhood experiences in the concentration camps of Auschwitz and Buchenwald. It includes an account of how one day following an incident a young boy is hanged in front of the inmates by way of restoring order. As the boy hangs dying on the gallows, someone shouts, "For God's sake, where is God?" And the narrator in the novel hears a voice inside himself saying, "This is where—hanging here from this gallows . . ."[8] This story has become famous as the only such account in modern Jewish literature of God being revealed in the death of a human being.

Of course, the prophets of ancient Israel suffered and died for the people and surely revealed God in their own ways (Jer 20:1–18; Mark 12:1–12; Heb 11:32–38). And there must have been thousands over the centuries who have done the same. But Wiesel's story is so like that of Jesus as to be shocking. On Good Friday, the basic questions come into sharp focus: How are we to understand the notion that God can be made known in pain, suffering, weakness, and death? And what is the message of Christians who claim that this is precisely what happened in the death of Jesus?

The idea that God is made known in human suffering can already be found in the book of Isaiah in the so-called Suffering Servant songs (42:1–4; 49:1–6; 50:4–9; and 52:13—53:12). The identity of the servant is unknown. Some think he might be an individual who represents Israel or that he is a personification of Israel itself or a part of Israel, a faithful remnant. But it is the theology that matters here. The idea of seeing God in suffering or of God being revealed in suffering permeates these texts. The major themes across the four songs in Isaiah are: he is chosen by God, he has humility and compassion, he is Spirit-endowed and persevering, he is a light and an

---

8. Wiesel, *Night*, 65.

example to all, and he is one who is obedient, endures pain and suffering on behalf of others, and in the end is vindicated. The suffering servant of Isaiah shows something of the humility of God himself: this is what God is like.

Christians soon saw in the suffering servant a prophecy of Jesus. Some New Testament texts are especially resonant with the idea of the servant: for example, the idea that Jesus came to serve rather than be served (Luke 22:24–27), that his death is a ransom for many (Mark 10:45), or that he suffered silently (1 Pet 2:22–25). In his First Letter to the Corinthians Paul writes, "For I decided to know nothing among you except Jesus Christ, and him crucified" (2:2). The Corinthians are to understand that the cross of Jesus lies at the center of Christian life and preaching. It is in the cross that the real message of the gospel can be seen. For Paul, human weakness is a real strength and the weakness of Christ is summed up in the cross. Indeed, this weakness is God's wisdom and power (1:24). The same fundamental message can be seen in Paul's Second Letter to the Corinthians when he again writes about weakness as strength (8:9; 12:10).

The cross is central again in Paul's Letter to the Philippians where he writes that Christ was humbled to death on a cross before being highly exalted by God (2:6–11). The so-called hymn is a summary statement of the basic idea that God brings exaltation out of suffering and death. Paul exhorts the Philippians to agree with one another and look out for the interests of others (2:1–5). Then, linking Christian behavior with the very nature of Christ's example, he refers to Christ's own humility, suffering, and death. Christ was "in the form of God" but humbled himself like a slave, in obedience, even to death on a cross. The cross is the center and also the basis of Paul's message. Because of this ultimate humility, God highly exalted Christ and gave him a name above all names. This has cosmic significance in God's purposes and forms the basis of how Paul thinks of Christ and of God: through suffering and death, God is revealed as one who is himself humble.

So, what are we to make of the claim that God is revealed in pain, suffering, and death? Why did a voice in Wiesel's novel claim to see God revealed in the death of a young boy in a concentration camp? And why do Christians continue to see God revealed in the death of Jesus? First of all, because in death we see something basic about humanity. We see mortality, createdness, innocence, weakness, and vulnerability. And the absence of God often mirrors his presence. We also see in death, the life a person has lived and the things they stood for. We see their lives and their ideals negated. And so we see God revealed in the place opposite to the power that is putting them to death. This power is usually the power of empire, the power of the world, and the power of abuse. It is in innocence, weakness, and vulnerability that we see something pure breaking through. The depths of humanity reflect sparks of divinity.

Elie Wiesel died in 2016 but his novel *Night* will remain a profound reflection on the horror of the Holocaust. The sense that God is revealed in the death of a young boy is powerful and shocking. The parallel with the Christian understanding of the death of Jesus is striking. There is a resonance here between something in the Jewish consciousness and something in Christianity. But, of course, the message of Good Friday indicates something more than God revealed in death: it points to the spark of new life breaking through. For Christians, the death of Jesus is also transfiguration and resurrection.

Bible Study Passages

Isa 52:13—53:12

Mark 10:45

1 Pet 2:22–25

Questions for Discussion

Share your response to Wiesel's account of God revealed in the death of a young boy.

Discuss the meaning of the Suffering Servant passages in Isaiah.

What is your understanding of Jesus' death?

How can Jesus' death be a "ransom for many" (Mark 10:45)?

How do suffering and pain show us something about God?

Further Reading

Young, Frances M. *Construing the Cross: Type, Sign, Symbol, Word, Action*. London: SPCK, 2016.

Wiesel, Elie. *Night*. London: Penguin, 2008.

Part 1: Through the Church's Year

GOOD FRIDAY (III): JESUS THE LAMB OF GOD

John Tavener is one of the best known of the twentieth-century English choral composers. His *Hymn to Athene* was sung at Princess Diana's funeral in Westminster Abbey in 1997. One of his other shorter and more famous pieces is his setting of William Blake's poem *The Lamb*. This has come to typify Tavener's style and character as a composer: a scintillating blend of traditional and modern harmony with just enough dissonance to enable the piece to become accepted in the popular market. It has gained quite considerable ground over the years after being chosen more than once as the modern piece sung at the annual Christmas Eve King's College Cambridge Festival of Nine Lessons and Carols. Gradually *The Lamb* has become fully accepted as a respected piece in the modern classical choral repertoire.[9]

Blake's poem, from his collection *Songs of Innocence*, is itself a reflection on creation and the place of Jesus Christ. In the first verse the lamb is asked if it knows who its maker is, drawing attention to its beauty. The second verse answers that the one who made the lamb is himself a lamb and so pointing out the parallels of meekness and humility between the lamb and Jesus. This verse reveals that it is a child speaking and points out how both the child and the lamb have a common name with Jesus who is creator and is both a child and a lamb. The theme is "Jesus the Lamb of God," an image used in the Eucharist and said frequently by Christians: "Lamb of God, you take away the sin of the world, have mercy on us." And then: "Jesus is the Lamb of God who takes away the sin of the world."[10] Where does the image of "Jesus the Lamb of God" come from and what does it mean?

In the Bible the idea that Jesus is the "Lamb of God" is found predominantly in St. John's gospel. It appears first in chapter 1 of the gospel in a striking and sudden way. The subject has been John the Baptist and his relation to Jesus and then the author says, "The next day he saw Jesus coming toward him and declared, 'Here is the Lamb of God who takes away the sin of the world!'" (1:29). Then a few verses later John uses this image of Jesus again: "Look, here is the Lamb of God!" (1:36).

More profound, perhaps, than the use of the expression "Lamb of God" for Jesus is the way in which the Fourth Gospel rearranges the timing of Jesus' death later in the gospel to coincide with the death of the Passover lambs. In the Synoptic Gospels (Matthew, Mark, and Luke) the Last Supper

---

9. For recordings of "The Lamb" and "Song to Athene," see Tavener, *Innocence*.
10. The words can be found in the Eucharist in most of the churches.

is a Passover meal (Matt 26:17; Mark 14:12; Luke 22:1) and Jesus dies on the cross the day following this. But in John's gospel we're specifically told that it was the Day of Preparation for the Passover when the disciples ate their last meal with Jesus (13:1; 19:31), indicating that the following day when he died would have been the day when the Passover lambs died in readiness for the Passover meal. In John's gospel, therefore, Jesus dies a day earlier and the effect is that he is portrayed as the Passover lamb whose death is the death of a lamb. The image, symbol, or metaphor is played out in the way the evangelist rearranges the timing of Jesus' death. It is also in evidence when Jesus is hanging on the cross and the soldiers do not break his legs because he is already dead (John 19:31–37). Here, he is being portrayed as the pure unblemished sacrificial animal, the lamb (cf. Exod 12, esp. v. 46; Lev 1:10–13; Num 9:12).

The background of the Lamb of God imagery is the sacrificial system of the Jerusalem temple. Both the temple of Solomon and the later temple of Herod the Great existed primarily for sacrifice. In the Jewish theology of the time, blood signified life (Gen 9:4; Lev 17:11, 14; Deut 12:23; cf. Heb 9:15–22). God had given life in creation and offering life back to God was considered a way of winning back his favor. Sacrifice was a way of dealing with sin or separation from God and when blood was taken from an animal, it was given back to God in thanksgiving. There were several different sorts of sacrifice (see Lev 1–7) but they were all related to making amends for sin. Different animals were used in sacrifice but the lamb was considered to be a pure animal and so a perfect sacrifice. Thus, when a lamb was offered in sacrifice, its blood was shed and poured upon the altar which was situated just outside the holy of holies in the temple. The theology is crucial: a bridge between humanity and God was built as a way of dealing with sin. The lamb itself was the bridge because it was the implement of eliminating sin.

This, then, is the background of calling Jesus the Lamb of God. It is a temple metaphor used to capture the fact that in Jesus people can find their way back to God; that separation from God (or sin) can be healed. It all turns on the concept of sacrifice and blood, as found in ancient Judaism. The culture we live in today is unfamiliar with this concept of blood sacrifice. It does not see blood in the same way as ancient Judaism although it is useful to remember that blood still indicates life. Today when we call Jesus the Lamb of God in our worship, we are using a metaphor that has lost its temple background and thus its meaning. It is important, therefore, to know what the background is if we are to understand what is being said about Jesus in this image and why it matters. The music of John Tavener and the poetry of William Blake remind us that there is a powerful background here. When we call Jesus the Lamb of God in church, it is important to appreciate its full meaning and implications.

Bible Study Passages

Lev 1:1–17

John 1:29–37

John 19:31–37

Questions for Discussion

What do you think the ancient Jewish sacrifices were all about?

Why was the lamb so important in sacrifices?

What sense does it make to call Jesus the "Lamb of God"?

Are there other metaphors that are more appropriate for Jesus?

How do you feel about using the "Lamb of God" idea in church services?

Further Reading

Blake, William. *Songs of Innocence and of Experience.* London: Folio, 1992.

Edwards, Ruth B. *Discovering John: Content, Interpretation, Reception.* London: SPCK, 2014.

HOLY SATURDAY: HOLY FIRE!

Every year in the Church of the Holy Sepulcher in Jerusalem on the day before Orthodox Easter Day there's a world-famous service known as "Holy Fire." It's a celebration of the resurrection of Jesus using fire and light as the main symbols and goes back to at least the ninth century. The service attracts thousands of people annually and is one of the most amazing events in Jerusalem at any time of the year. Weeks beforehand there's competition to get in as it's a tickets-only event. And even with a ticket you might not actually make it! These days the occasion is strictly managed by the Israeli Police, and safety and crowd control are the order of the day.

When the day for Holy Fire comes, there's great excitement. People make their way to the church very early in the morning and wait several hours for the service to begin. The focus is on the tomb of Christ under the main dome of the church. When the moment arrives, the Greek and Armenian Patriarchs of Jerusalem go into the tomb and the door is sealed. Then the "miracle of the holy fire" takes place and the flame emerges from holes in the side of the tomb. An Armenian priest appears high on a balcony above the tomb holding a burning candle in the air as the candles of thousands of pilgrims are lit. Orthodox pilgrims bathe their faces in the flames, and lanterns containing the fire are hurried to Tel Aviv airport to be flown directly to Istanbul (ancient Constantinople) and Moscow, the capital cities of the Orthodox world. Holy Fire is an extraordinary service bringing home to everyone present the importance of the symbols of fire and light.

The fire of Holy Fire symbolizes the resurrection of Jesus. Being an elemental symbol (earth, fire, air, and water) it has a primordial impact. Fire indicates light, warmth, and growth which are all essential for physical life. Fire and light are, therefore, both powerful symbols of the religious and spiritual life. They speak to people across nations and cultures, and bring home the power and strength of the new life that comes through Jesus' resurrection.

In the Hebrew Bible, fire is a regular feature. God appears to Moses in the fire of the Burning Bush (Exod 3:2) and on Mount Sinai (Exod 19:18). When the Israelites are wandering forty years in the desert, God commands them to light a perpetual light in the tent of meeting (Exod 27:20; Lev 24:1–4) and they're guided by a pillar of fire at night (Exod 13:21). There's fire when Solomon dedicates the temple in Jerusalem (2 Chr 7:1–3) and the action of God is symbolized by fire when Elijah wins the competition with the prophets of Baal on Mount Carmel: God sends down fire to consume the sacrifice (1 Kgs 18:20–40). God himself is sometimes depicted as having fire in his mouth (2 Sam 22:9; Ps 18:8) and there's often fire where there are angels (Judg 6:21; 13:20; Dan 10:6), and in the heavenly realm (Rev 1:14; 2:18).

The second side of the Holy Fire symbol is "light," an even more significant symbol in the Bible. In the book of Genesis, light is created by God in the separation of day and night (1:1–5). It is part of God's creative life-giving act. On the first day of creation as he separates light from darkness he says, "Let there be light" and there is (1:3 cf. 1:14–19). Elsewhere in the Hebrew Bible, light is the shining of God's presence and action, the radiance of God's glory (Isa 60:1–3), and the illumination of human life. In Proverbs 13:9 we read, "The light of the righteous rejoices, but the lamp of the wicked goes out." And in Psalm 36:9 God's light is the light in which everything else can be seen.

Fire and light are also used as symbols in the New Testament. The Holy Spirit comes on the apostles at Pentecost like tongues of fire (Acts 2:3) and fire is a symbol of God's judgment (1 Cor 4:5). Then, in John's gospel Jesus himself is the light of the world contrasted with the darkness that cannot overcome it (John 1:1–14; 8:12). Elsewhere, he is a light to the Gentiles (Luke 2:32), and his disciples are the "light of the world" (Matt 5:14), and "children of light" (Luke 16:8). Christians stand in God's light (1 Tim 6:16; 1 Pet 2:9) and for Paul, God is one who brings light out of darkness (2 Cor 4:6). In the book of Revelation, light is a symbol of God's presence at the end of time (21:23–24; 22:5). And in the famous Dead Sea Scrolls, light imagery appears especially in the text known as the *War of the Sons of Light Against the Sons of Darkness*, which envisages a final cosmic battle between good and evil or light and darkness.[11]

The famous service of Holy Fire in the Church of the Holy Sepulcher in Jerusalem is an amazing experience for all who attend. The effect of the symbols of fire and light is really striking and the centuries-old service enhances the sense of Christ's risen life in everyone present. Following the service, pilgrims and locals leave the church carrying their flames of "new fire" in individual lanterns. The service of Holy Fire can be held anywhere in the world and indeed often is, in cathedrals and local churches. In using the symbols of fire and light for the resurrection of Jesus it draws on a primordial element within us and carries all the nuances of new life: warmth, growth, seeing, leading, guiding, nurturing, and comforting. Easter itself is a celebration of God's creative act of overcoming darkness, sin, and guilt, of his re-creating humanity through new birth and new life, and of his constant drawing of the whole creation into his ultimate purposes for us in the resurrection. Fire and light symbolize those things. In so many different ways the service of Holy Fire, wherever it takes place, is a really powerful reminder of the new life we share in Christ.

---

11. See Vermes, *Dead Sea Scrolls*, 161–89.

Bible Study Passages

Exod 3:1–6

John 8:12

2 Cor 4:6

Questions for Discussion

Why are light and darkness so powerful?

Discuss the strengths and weaknesses of fire as a religious symbol.

Where are images of fire and light used in the Bible and how successful are they?

What does it mean to say that Jesus is the "light of the world"?

Share your experiences of using fire as an image in church.

Further Reading

Greene-McCreight, Kathryn. *I Am With You*. London: Bloomsbury, 2015.

Novakovic, Lidija. *Resurrection: A Guide for the Perplexed*. London: Bloomsbury, 2016.

EASTER DAY: THE GARDEN OF GOD

Having an Easter Garden in church during Eastertide is a wonderful idea. Between Easter Day and Ascension Day (forty days later) you'll often see a model of the empty tomb of Jesus in a garden, usually set up on a table, on the floor or under an altar in church. These model gardens have appeared in churches in England since Victorian times and can now be found in many different countries around the world. The basics are as follows: an empty tomb made out of stones with the main stone rolled away and maybe grave cloths lying visible inside; a cross (or possibly three) nearby; a figure of the risen Jesus outside the tomb; and one of Mary Magdalene close by. Also, two angels sitting outside the tomb. There are usually plenty of plants and flowers, and the imagination can run wild with the number of rocks, stones, and pathways that are included. The Easter Garden is really fun to construct, not least when children (of all ages!) get involved. The idea is to provide a colorful reminder of the resurrection of Jesus and a visible focus for prayer and meditation for worshippers.

Although Easter Gardens can be based on any of the gospel accounts of the resurrection, the main account is the appearance of Jesus to Mary Magdalene in John 20:1–18. This story isn't in the Synoptic Gospels and differs substantially from the empty tomb stories in Matthew (28:1–10), Mark (16:1–8), and Luke (24:1–12). Mary Magdalene (who does appear in the other empty tomb stories) comes to the tomb early and sees the stone rolled away (v. 1). She immediately tells Simon Peter and the beloved disciple, and they run to the tomb (vv. 2–3). The beloved disciple gets to the tomb before Peter and they see the linen cloths lying inside (vv. 4–9). They then leave but Mary remains outside the tomb crying (vv. 10–11). Two angels appear (signifying divine presence) and she tells them what has happened (vv. 12–13). Then she turns around and sees Jesus (v. 14). The gospel writer says: "Supposing him to be the gardener, she said to him, 'Sir, if you have carried him away, tell me where you have laid him, and I will take him away'" (v. 15). Jesus speaks Mary's name and she recognizes him (v. 16) and then goes to the disciples with a message from him (vv. 17–18). Probably the most moving of all the resurrection appearance stories, this encounter has been painted by Rembrandt, Fra Angelico, and Titian, among many others.

There are several very important themes in this story: the focus, of course, is the resurrection and the nature of discipleship. But a fundamental aspect, usually overlooked, is the setting: the garden itself. Unlike the other evangelists, the writer of the Fourth Gospel has already alluded to creation and the garden of Eden in Genesis by opening his gospel with a reminder about God the creator: "In the beginning . . ." (Gen 1:1; John 1:1). He has also taken the trouble to place Jesus' betrayal, crucifixion, and burial in gardens (John 18:1; 19:41). Now, in the story of the appearance to Mary Magdalene the writer thinks it important to mention that she thinks Jesus is the gardener. The garden theme is clearly important and worth bringing out.

Once the garden has been pointed out, it's not difficult to appreciate the connection between the garden of the resurrection here in the Johannine story and the garden of Eden in Genesis. The garden in Genesis is the primordial garden, the garden of paradise, and the garden where the first human beings are created and where God walks quietly. This garden symbolizes God's power as creator alongside his original intentions for human beings. In later Christian thinking, especially after Augustine's theology of the fall, it came to symbolize original perfection but even without that, it might indicate original innocence. The garden of Eden is the beginning, how God originally wanted things to be.

The background in ancient Near Eastern literature is also significant. Gardens were associated with the gods and with divine power, with kings and queens, royal families, wealth, and fertility. The famous Hanging Gardens of Babylon (whether real or imaginary) and the Assyrian Hanging Garden at Nineveh have these associations. Water, trees, and plants are symbolic of paradise. The symbolism is there in Jerusalem itself where Solomon watered his gardens from the Gihon spring. This is the city of God where earth and heaven meet. Thereafter, wherever trees and plants are mentioned, the image of the garden is present, conjuring up divinity, wealth, wisdom, royalty, fertility, and power: the coming of God to earth. The symbolism is taken up by the postexilic prophet Ezekiel who in his vision of the New Jerusalem sees water pouring out from the Holy City, watering the garden of the end of time. He calls this the "garden of God" (28:13; 31:8–9). It is the garden where God dwells and where the divinity is made known. The original garden of perfection and innocence has become the end-time garden of perfection.

The appearance of Jesus in a garden in John 20, therefore, is of great significance. It's not just a throwaway line—that Mary thinks he's the gardener. In many respects he really is the gardener, because he stands risen in God's garden which is the new Eden and the place where things in creation are finally as they ought to be. The garden is the setting of the beginning and of the end, of God's original and ultimate purposes in creation. Just as things began in purity and innocence so they now end in the new garden were things are brought to perfection by God in the resurrection of Jesus. Theologically, this shows a very important connection between the processes of creation, resurrection, and the end of time.

Having an Easter Garden in church during Eastertide is a wonderful thing. It's not just a colorful decoration for those who like that sort of thing. It reminds worshippers of the connection between the resurrection of Jesus and God's purposes in the whole of creation. It points visibly to the beginning and end of creation, and to the sense that the resurrection of Jesus lifts everything into a new state of completion. The Easter Garden is a powerful icon for the whole season.

Part 1: Through the Church's Year

Bible Study Passages

Gen 2:1–17

John 19:38–42

John 20:1–18

Questions for Discussion

What is so special about gardens?

Share some of your experiences of gardens.

What is the significance of the garden of Eden?

How important is it that Jesus appears to Mary Magdalene in a garden?

What is the "theology of the garden" in John's gospel?

Further Reading

Dennis, Trevor. *The Easter Stories*. London: SPCK, 2008.

Williams, Rowan. *Choose Life: Christmas and Easter Sermons in Canterbury Cathedral*. London: Bloomsbury, 2013.

ASCENSION DAY: DON'T CLING TO ME

Every year on Ascension Day in Jerusalem, Christians assemble in the early morning on the Mount of Olives to celebrate the feast. They gather in a small octagonal building that's been a mosque since 1187 when Saladin took the city from the Crusaders and ended the Latin kingdom. As in many places in the Holy Land, the Crusader church stood on the site of an earlier Byzantine building. And the famous pilgrim Egeria went to the Mount of Olives in the fourth century for an Ascension Day liturgy. The present-day building sits at the highest point on the Mount of Olives and is known locally as the *Imbomon* (from the Greek *en bommo* meaning "on the hill"). Inside there's a *mihrab* indicating the direction of Mecca to the south and in the floor a rectangular stone showing an alleged footprint of Jesus. This building is the Mosque or Chapel of the Ascension. Both Christians and Muslims celebrate the ascension of Jesus but its meaning often remains elusive.

I can only speak about the place of the ascension of Jesus in Christianity. It is more important than is often thought: it's mentioned in the Nicene and Apostles' Creeds which are recited regularly by Christians, and is celebrated annually by Christians in churches all over the world. It is generally reckoned to be one of the major feasts of the church and is always kept forty days after Easter (following Acts 1:3, though cf. Luke 24:36–53 which implies it was on the same day as the resurrection) marking the official end of Eastertide. In the New Testament the story occurs only in Luke's gospel (24:50–53) and Acts (1:9–11) but ascension language permeates other texts, not least St. John's gospel.

The most important ascension text in the Gospel of John is Jesus' resurrection appearance to Mary Magdalene (20:11–18). When she finally recognizes who he is, he says to her, "Do not hold on to me, because I have not yet ascended to the Father. But go to my brothers and say to them, 'I am ascending to my Father and your Father, to my God and your God'" (v. 17). At that very moment, it seems, Jesus is in the process of ascending and Mary must not attempt to hang on to his physical body. Now, following the resurrection, a new, nonphysical relationship with him is possible and Mary is encouraged not to try to hang on, even to Jesus' risen body. Resurrection and ascension are clearly interrelated here but belong to two different stages: ascension takes resurrection further, beyond past identities and beyond the physical.

Other ascension-related language earlier in John's gospel shows how important the ascension is and how it is interrelated with other stages of Jesus' life. The evangelist writes about Jesus "ascending and descending," about him being "lifted up" and "going to the Father." The pattern begins, of course, when "the Word became flesh" (1:1–14). Then there's Jacob's Ladder and angels ascending and descending on the Son of Man (1:51), the Bread of Life discourse where Jesus talks about the bread coming down and the Son of Man ascending (6:38, 62), and the language of "lifting up" and glorification which refers, sometimes ambiguously, to the crucifixion and/or resurrection (3:13–15; 8:28; 12:23, 32). References to Jesus "going to the Father" refer perhaps more obviously to the ascension (16:7, 28; 17:11, 13).

Through this spatial imagery, the fourth evangelist shows how Jesus' life, death, resurrection, and ascension are all part of God's continuous "raising" of Jesus. The descending and ascending are part of the broader movement of God's action in Jesus from the beginning. By the end, the ascension indicates the ultimate divine approval of everything Jesus has done.

Following the resurrection, he is taken fully into the life of God and the physical is transcended, though not denied. Mary is not to hang on to past experiences of Jesus but to move forward into a new relationship with him. Within the overall pattern, the physical is taken up but now transcended.

Other New Testament texts also use ascension language without actually describing the event. Paul speaks of Christ being "highly exalted" (Phil 2:9) and at the "right hand of God" (Rom 8:34) as well as using ascending-descending language (Eph 4:8–10). The Epistle to the Hebrews says Jesus "passed through the heavens" (4:14), 1 Timothy says he was "taken up in glory" (3:16) and 1 Peter says he has "gone into heaven" (3:22). For some New Testament writers, Christians are also caught up in the ascension of Jesus (John 14:2–3; 1 Thess 4:17) and a new relationship is again envisaged.

The annual liturgical celebrations on Ascension Day at the *Imbomon* on the Mount of Olives in Jerusalem are exciting and colorful. They attract local people as well as pilgrims from far and wide. They draw attention to something in Christian faith which needs more attention than it often gets. Ultimately, this important festival celebrates another phase in the continuous sweep of God's purposes in Jesus, beginning with the incarnation and including his life, death, and resurrection. All this can be thought of as a descending-ascending movement of God's love for us as he embraces creation but moves us beyond it. In the ascension, Jesus is taken up into God's life and a new nonphysical relationship with him is made possible. Mary Magdalene is asked not to hold on to the Jesus she has known in the past, and not to cling to comfortable and familiar experiences of him. She is challenged to embrace a new dimension of faith which affirms the physical but draws her forward beyond it.

And this alerts us to the fact that the ascension isn't just a story about Jesus' disappearance but an important part of the way we think of God's dealings with the world. Like Mary, we are also challenged to let go of the physical and the familiar and be open to the ascended Jesus who pulls us ever upward toward the Spirit: Ascension Day then leads on to Pentecost.

Bible Study Passages

Luke 24:36–53 and Acts 1:6–11

John 20:11–18

Phil 2:6–11

Questions for Discussion

What is your understanding of the ascension of Jesus?

Why do you think the ascension story is only in Luke-Acts?

Discuss the "ascending-descending" language of St. John's gospel.

Why does Jesus ask Mary not to cling to him in John 20:17?

Is the ascension of Jesus as important as his resurrection? Explain.

Further Reading

Bauckham, Richard. *Gospel of Glory: Major Themes in Johannine Theology*. Grand Rapids: Baker, 2015.

Johnson, Luke Timothy. *The Creed: What Christians Believe and Why It Matters*. London: Darton, Longman & Todd, 2003.

4

Pentecost and Trinity

PARACLETE: TESTED IN THE FIRE

"Come, thou holy Paraclete."[1] The opening words of the thirteenth-century Pentecost hymn known as the "Golden Sequence." At Pentecost or Whitsun all the Holy Spirit hymns come out for their annual airing in church services. And there are some really moving ones: "Come Down, O Love Divine"; "Come, Holy Ghost, Our Souls Inspire"; "Breathe on Me, Breath of God"; "Spirit of the Living God, Fall Afresh on Me," and many more.[2] But "Come, Thou Holy Paraclete"? That's an unusual word for the Holy Spirit: "Paraclete." The Holy Spirit does get called a number of different things in hymns and worship, and many of them are familiar in other contexts: advocate, comforter, counsellor. Different words are already used in the Bible for the breath or spirit of God. "Paraclete" isn't one you normally hear in any other walk of life but it's there in the New Testament though only in St. John's gospel. At Pentecost, it's worth looking at this very unusual word a bit more closely.

In St. John's gospel, the Holy Spirit is mentioned several times (1:33; 14:26; 20:22) but the actual teaching about the Spirit uses the word Paraclete and this occurs in chapters 14–16. English translations of the gospel use words such as advocate, comforter, or counsellor but the Greek is Paraclete. This word can, in fact, be translated as advocate, comforter, counsellor, consoler, helper, spokesman, or witness. The problem is that the word has a broad range of possible meanings which makes translation difficult.

---

1. See Vaughan Williams, *English Hymnal*, no. 155.
2. All these other hymns can be found in Barnard, *Ancient & Modern*.

Sometimes translators give up and simply transliterate: the Greek *parakletos* becomes "Paraclete." Literally, the Greek means "one who is called alongside" basically that is "to help." The background to the word can be found in the law courts. It's a forensic or judicial word. The Paraclete is an accuser or a witness to the truth, one who is brought in alongside others to bear witness to truth and to challenge and test. The word is taken up by the author of the Fourth Gospel to draw out the deeper meaning of the role of the Holy Spirit. It is very noticeable that this is the fourth evangelist's chosen and preferred word for the Holy Spirit, and that one of the things the Paraclete will do is challenge and test.

The word Paraclete occurs in four passages in St. John's gospel: 14:15–17; 14:26; 15:26–27; 16:7–15.[3] These all fall in the section known as the Farewell Discourses and give quite a bit of detail about the work of the Paraclete. The first passage comes soon after the supper scene in which Jesus washes his disciples' feet, giving them an example of love (13:1–20) and commanding them to love one another (13:34). Then he adds that if they love him, the Father will send "another Paraclete" to be with them for ever (14:16), indicating that Jesus is the first Paraclete. The one who will come is also called the "Spirit of truth" (14:17; cf. 15:26). He continues Jesus' work after Jesus' departure. The world doesn't know this one but the disciples know him because he dwells in them. The second passage (14:26) refers to the Paraclete as a teacher, one who will remind them of what Jesus has told them. The third passage (15:26–27) tells that the Paraclete will bear witness to Jesus as the disciples themselves must. And finally, in 16:7–15 we are told that unless Jesus goes away, the Paraclete will not come and that Jesus will send him. There are then three specific things that the Paraclete will do: he will "prove the world wrong about sin and righteousness and judgement" (16:8). The actual task of the Paraclete is twofold: he will be with the disciples, teaching and guiding them; and he will put the world to the test.

All this bears on the way in which we are to imagine the "Spirit-Paraclete" (as it is often known). The coming of the Paraclete after Jesus' departure brings to mind a basic biblical pattern in which authority and responsibility are handed over from one person to another. For example, Moses hands over to Joshua before the entry of the people of Israel into the promised land (Deut 34). Elijah hands over to Elisha as he ascends into

---

3. The KJV has "Comforter," the RSV has "Counsellor," and the NEB has "Advocate." The NRSV has "Advocate" with "Paraclete" in a footnote. I have kept the original Greek word "Paraclete" in the text here.

heaven (2 Kgs 2:1–15). John the Baptist hands over to Jesus as he himself disappears (John 1:19–34; 3:30). And Jesus hands over to the "Spirit-Paraclete" as he passes through death and resurrection. The emphasis in the Fourth Gospel is that the Paraclete continues what Jesus himself has done and stood for, and continues with the disciples as Jesus' presence in the world. Part of the Paraclete's role is to teach, test, and challenge those whom he comes alongside.

The word Paraclete is a powerful if unusual word. It was John Mason Neale, the famous nineteenth-century translator of "Come, Thou Holy Paraclete," who turned the Latin *spiritus* in the thirteenth-century hymn into "Paraclete." In the hymn, the Paraclete is thought of as a light-giver and comforter, a purifier and strengthener. And we often think of the Holy Spirit today largely in terms of comfort and strength. But in the Gospel of John the word Paraclete suggests something much more serious and demanding. Here the word has a variety of different meanings and associations. Here it is another Jesus, one whom Jesus sends from God to carry on the things he has been doing. He is one who "comes alongside" as a teacher to test, challenge, and judge. His role is even to confront those alongside whom he comes with sinfulness and righteousness. Indeed, although the Paraclete is a comforter in one sense it is not in the sense of ease and leisure. The comfort given by the Paraclete is a testing and purifying process which suggests hard work with effort and concentration. The message for Pentecost today is surely that the Paraclete requires of us a response that is in keeping with our calling. We are to be strengthened and comforted, yes, but also tested in the fire, refined and challenged to be more like Jesus and to follow in his way.

Bible Study Passages

John 14:15–17 and 26

John 15:26–27

John 16:7–15

Questions for Discussion

What do you understand by the word "Paraclete"?

What is the difference between the Holy Spirit and the Paraclete?

What does the Paraclete do in St. John's gospel?

What is your experience of the Holy Spirit?

How useful is the word "Paraclete" in Christian worship today?

Further Reading

Lincoln, Andrew T. *The Gospel according to St. John*. Grand Rapids: Baker, 2013.

Williams, Jane, ed. *The Holy Spirit in the World Today*. London: Alpha, 2011.

PENTECOST: EL GRECO

One of the most famous paintings by the sixteenth-century artist El Greco (real name Domenikos Theotokopoulos) is the one depicting the day of Pentecost as recounted in Acts 2:1–4. Known simply as *Pentecost*, the painting was originally the center of a five-panel altar piece in the Colegio de Dona Maria de Aragon, a seminary in Madrid. It is oil on canvas and has been in the Prado in Madrid since the time of Napoleon. El Greco (1541–1614) was born in Crete but moved to Spain via Italy where he may have studied with Titian in Venice. He then made his way to Madrid and Toledo. Influenced by Greek Byzantine icon painting and the Venetian schools of his own day, he has influenced many artists since. Painted about 1600, *Pentecost* is instantly recognizable as El Greco: the vivid colors, the elongated figures and an element of mysticism. And in this painting, there's fire and wind bringing to life the event of the coming of the Holy Spirit on Mount Zion in Jerusalem.

El Greco's painting is alive with color. At the top a dove symbolizes the Holy Spirit descending from heaven in a ray of sunlight. The long slim figures gather around the Virgin Mary. There are fifteen figures: twelve apostles, plus Mary the Mother of Jesus and then another Mary (possibly Magdalene or the mother of James or perhaps it's the patron of the painting). And then the face of El Greco himself! On each figure is a flame of fire as in the account in Acts. The Holy Spirit came in "divided tongues, as of fire." The painting also captures the sense of "the rush of a violent wind" in the way garments are swirling and figures moving (Acts 2:2–3). The painting captures the dynamic movement of the Spirit's descent and something of the joining of heaven and earth in the whole drama of the scene. This is the beginning of the church, the origins of the new community in Christ's name. Indeed, it is the birth of the church whose origins and purpose are Spirit filled and Spirit led.

We often think of Pentecost as the Holy Spirit "coming down" but it is also important to remember that it "takes us up" with it. In the Old Testament it is noticeable that the Spirit is connected to some of the key moments in God's creation of the world. First, it's there at the beginning of Genesis, where "a wind from God swept over the face of the waters" (1:2). It's part of God's way of creating and shaping the world he is making. The same idea can be seen in the book of Job where Elihu says, "The spirit of God has made me, and the breath of the Almighty gives me life" (33:4). In Psalm 104:30 all parts of creation look to God, and the writer says, "When you send forth your spirit, they are created; and you renew the face of the ground." The Spirit is certainly active in creation. It is also active in the lives of specific individuals such as judges (Judg 3:10) and kings like David (1 Sam 16:13). The Spirit is upon the servant in Isaiah 42:1 and upon prophets throughout Israel's history (Neh 9:30; Ezek 2:2; Mic 3:8). It inspires and drives people in their service of God. Significantly it is also connected with ideas about the end of time (Isa 11:1–2; Ezek 39:29). In Joel 2:28–29 the prophet sees the Spirit poured out on all flesh at the end of time. Thus, God uses his Spirit to lift up and perfect the whole of creation from the beginning, in the lives of significant people and at the end of time.

These themes continue in the New Testament, especially in Luke's gospel and Acts. The Holy Spirit is mentioned in relation to John the Baptist at the beginning of Luke at Zechariah's vision in the temple in Jerusalem (1:15). The Holy Spirit is there at the conception of Jesus (1:35) and at his baptism (3:22), and it is the Spirit that leads him into the desert to be tempted by Satan (4:1). At the beginning of Jesus' ministry in Nazareth he quotes Isaiah 61:1, "The Spirit of the Lord is upon me" (4:18) and it is the Spirit that is to replace Jesus when he departs (24:49). The Spirit then comes on the day of Pentecost in Acts when it appears like a rush of mighty wind and in tongues of fire (2:1–13) as in El Greco's painting. It then continues to play a part throughout the story of the emerging church (Acts 4:8; 5:3; 8:29; 20:23). The Spirit also plays a key role in John's gospel (mostly as the Paraclete: 14:15–17, 26; 15:26–27; 16:7–15) where it replaces Jesus. And it plays a fundamental role in the theology of St. Paul (e.g., Rom 8:1–17; Gal 3:1–5; 5:22–23). Throughout all of this, the Spirit not only "comes down" but "takes up" those under its influence.

What then can be learned from the many biblical texts and from El Greco's painting when we put them together? We see that the Holy Spirit comes from God to lift up the whole of creation. It's there at crucial moments of creation, inspiration, and completion. God works through his Spirit in creating, fashioning, and refining. The Day of Pentecost in Acts is, to be sure, a special pouring out of the Spirit, but this is a particular case of what God is always doing everywhere. And as the Spirit is poured out and comes down, creation and everything in it is taken up into God's purposes. Certainly, the El Greco painting captures this theme: the Holy Spirit isn't just "coming down" from above; the apostles are being raised up from below. Their bodies are portrayed as elongated figures raising their arms in prayer, swirling upward toward the divine realm. This is the mystical element typical of El Greco's paintings in which earth and heaven meet. Indeed, Pentecost is a celebration of the Holy Spirit lifting the whole of creation into the life of God and bringing earth up to heaven.

Bible Study Passages

Gen 1:1–2

Acts 2:1–13

Rom 8:9–11

Questions for Discussion

What does the feast of Pentecost celebrate?

Share your experiences of the Holy Spirit.

To what extent is the Holy Spirit absent before Pentecost?

What does it mean to say that the Holy Spirit "takes us up" into God?

In what sense is Pentecost the "beginning of the church"?

Further Reading

Thiselton, Anthony C. *A Shorter Guide to the Holy Spirit: Bible, Doctrine, Experience*. Grand Rapids: Eerdmans, 2016.

Twelftree, Graham. *People of the Spirit: Exploring Luke's View of the Church*. Grand Rapids: Baker, 2000.

Part 1: Through the Church's Year

TRIUNITY: THE TRIANGULAR LODGE

Deep in the Northamptonshire countryside, just outside Kettering near Leicester in England, about a mile from the Rushton Hall Spa Hotel, stands the amazing and fascinating "Rushton Triangular Lodge" built in the sixteenth century by Sir Thomas Tresham (1545–1605).[4] The lodge is a witness in stone to the Holy Trinity. Tresham was a staunch Roman Catholic during the period of the English Reformation and was imprisoned more than once for his beliefs. He built the lodge between 1594–1597 as a physical statement of his Catholic belief and commitment. It's a small but significant treasure still standing in a Northamptonshire field and is well worth a visit. It's also a colorful reminder of a fundamental aspect of Christian faith: the many-sidedness of God's ways with the world.

The Lodge is an equilateral triangle measuring 33.3 feet on each side. In addition to its three sides it has three floors and three gables on each side. It is crowned by a three-sided chimney. Trefoil windows characterize the building and there are triangles decorating it everywhere. Each side of the lodge has reference to one of the three persons of the Holy Trinity: Father, Son, and Holy Spirit. There are inscriptions with thirty-three letters and one over a doorway which reads *Tres Testimonium Dant* ("there are three that bear testimony"). This is a reference to 1 John 5:7 which reads, "There are three that testify in heaven, the Father, the Word, and the Holy Spirit, and these three are one." It is also a partial pun on Tresham's name (Tres). The lodge is made of red and cream sandstone and limestone giving a striped Byzantine effect. On a practical level, it was used by Tresham's rabbit keeper! Today it still stands as an architectural icon of the Trinity.

By Tresham's day, the notion of God as Trinity was well established in Christianity. Its roots lay in early Christian experience and it is reflected in the New Testament (see Matt 3:16; 28:19; Luke 1:35; John 14:11, 16–17, 26; 1 Cor 12:4–6; 2 Cor 13:13; 2 Thess 2:13–14; 1 Pet 1:2; Jude 20–21). The threefold nature of God had also been debated across several of the early Christian councils amid great controversy (Nicaea, 325 CE, on the divinity of the Son, and Constantinople, 381 CE, on the divinity of the Holy Spirit). During the Reformation period the Trinity remained central to Christian belief although in the shifting theological sands of the period it was challenged quite radically by some, especially those who believed in the strict unity of God and who became known as Unitarians. Tresham wanted to

---

4. See Isham, *Rushton*.

affirm his trinitarian faith in concrete terms and his design and construction of this extraordinary building seemed to fit the bill.

In recent decades, the idea of God as Trinity has become problematic to some, especially preachers and teachers, so it's a good idea, first of all, to find new language. "Trinity" and "The Doctrine of the Trinity," it is often claimed, sound a bit daunting and off-putting, and it's important to remember that the language was originally rooted in experience rather than in rational thinking. Because of this, people often talk these days about the "triunity" of God or about God as "triune" and there's much to be said in favor of this. The "triune God" has a more experiential feel about it and helps us imagine a God whose presence among us is many-sided.

Tresham chose the biblical text for his Lodge from 1 John 5:7 and it is certainly in the writings of John, especially the Gospel of John, that we find a great deal of the language which came to form the basis of thinking of God as "triune." It's John's gospel that tells us that God and the Logos or Word are together and even identified, and that the "Word became flesh" and dwelt on earth (1:1–14). The language of the Spirit, counsellor or advocate is also frequently encountered (14:15–17; 14:26; 15:26–27; 16:7–15). The three dimensions of Father, Word (or Son), and Spirit are undoubtedly part of the overall message of this gospel.

But it is in the life and writings of St. Paul that we find God's many-sidedness more clearly reflected as an experience. It's often debated whether Paul believed in the Trinity or even thought in such terms. But there's certainly a strong trinitarian undertow in his letters. As a Jew, he had a deep-seated experience of the God of Abraham, Isaac, and Jacob. And he eventually had a radical turnaround experience of Jesus in his famous Damascus Road experience (Acts 9:1–9; 22:1–11; 26:12–18). This experience showed Paul something new about God. It showed him the Jesus who did not count equality with God a thing to be grasped but was humbled to death (Phil 2:6–11) and the Jesus who was rich but became poor (2 Cor 8:9). No wonder Paul writes about Jesus as God's wisdom (1 Cor 1:24) and image (Col 1:15). For Paul, it seems, God and Jesus are fundamentally intertwined in his experience and thinking. And he certainly also knew of the power of God's Holy Spirit and its influence on Christian life (Rom 8:1–17; Gal 3:1–5; 5:22–23). Although Paul may not say it in philosophical terms, he certainly experienced and knew the triune God.

When Sir Thomas Tresham built the Rushton Triangular Lodge in Northamptonshire, England, he wished to affirm his faith in the many different sides of the God he experienced. He saw that element of his faith as central and worth making a statement about. Today the Rushton Lodge is still a witness to the many-sidedness of God's coming among us. Tresham left behind a "theology in stone" reminding us of the important place of the triune God in Christian experience, faith, and worship. And that triunity consists of God's very life breathing through us, coming from the Father, colored by the life of Jesus and energized by the Holy Spirit. Trinity Sunday is a day for celebrating the many different ways in which God's life permeates ours, the many different sides of his character, and the many different dimensions through which we can experience him. If you ever get chance to visit the Rushton Triangular Lodge in Northamptonshire, it's worth more than a look!

Bible Study Passages

Matt 28:16–20

Col 1:15–20

1 John 5:6–12

Questions for Discussion

How important is Trinity Sunday?

What is your experience of the Holy Trinity?

What do you know about the theology of the Trinity?

What are your feelings about Tresham's Triangular Lodge?

What would be a good way of celebrating Trinity Sunday?

Further Reading

Collins, Paul M. *The Trinity: A Guide for the Perplexed.* London: T. & T. Clark, 2008.

Letham, Robert. *The Holy Trinity: In Scripture, History, Theology, and Worship.* New Jersey: Presbyterian and Reformed, 2012.

PENTECOST AND TRINITY

TRINITY SUNDAY: GOD'S TWO HANDS

Finding the best language for talking about God can be really challenging. And finding the best images for the Holy Trinity gets even more complicated. How can we depict the various sides of God's nature in human language? And how can we truly reflect his triunity in images or pictures? By definition, all language, symbols, and metaphors for God fall short of what they're trying to do.

And yet, over the centuries, there have been many colorful attempts to portray God's threefold character using as illustrations or analogies things that are three and at the same time one. For example, water, ice, and steam, or the sun, its light, and its rays. There's also the famous shamrock or three-leaved flower associated with St. Patrick's preaching to the people of Ireland. It has three leaves but is also one, just like the clover leaf. Another well-known but more complicated image comes from the famous African theologian St. Augustine of Hippo (AD 354–439), the so-called psychological analogy. In fact, Augustine has two analogies for the Trinity using the human mind: "mind, knowledge, and love"; and "memory, understanding, and will." There's one mind but three aspects.[5] All these analogies have their strengths and weaknesses and there will probably never be a perfect image for helping us understand God as Trinity. However, one less well-known image is earlier than Augustine and comes from St. Irenaeus of Lyons (ca. AD 130–ca. 200). He writes of the Son and the Holy Spirit as God the Father's "two hands."[6] This is a vivid and powerful image with some real strengths.

Irenaeus was one of the most important Christian theologians of his time. The later "doctrine of the Trinity" in all its philosophical complexity had not yet been fully articulated in his day. That was to happen in the fourth and fifth centuries. But experience of God was already rooted in images of Father, Son, and Spirit and there were many attempts to express this in useful images. Irenaeus' image of God and his two hands is very striking. He doesn't explain the idea; he just uses it. The image of two hands captures the threefold aspect of God as well as the unity. It's simple and obvious: in a fully grown healthy human being there's one individual but two hands. Hands are important. We do important things with them. Irenaeus uses the image of God's hands when he's writing about God's activity in the world.

---

5. See Augustine, *De Trinitate*, bks. IX, X, and XIV, 314–15, 336–37, and 445–46.

6. See Irenaeus, *Against Heresies*, e.g., III.21.10; IV.19.2; 20.1; and V.1.3, 246, 302–3, 374.

The "two hands" image captures a creative, active element. It's anything but an abstraction.

In order to get a better sense of the two hands of God it's worth considering the other words Irenaeus uses in relation to them. The Son of God, he who was incarnate in Jesus was in Irenaeus' thinking also the Logos. This is pretty standard thinking of the time. The Logos concept is Greek but came to Christians through its use in St. John's gospel (1:1–18). We're told there that the Logos, the rational principle of the universe, was in the beginning with God: he was both "with God" and "was God" (1:1). He also became flesh in Jesus (1:14). It is not widely known that the Hebrew word behind the word Logos is *dabar*, which is a much more active concept. When prophets write, "The word of the Lord came to . . ." (e.g., Ezek 1:3), it is an active word, a word about doing something constructive. And indeed, the use of the Word of God in Christian trinitarian theology should be thought of as an activity rather than something static. In fact, St. John already points out that the Logos is God's instrument of creation: "Without him not one thing came into being" (1:3). This was taken up later in Christian theology and became very important in trinitarian thinking. So it is for Irenaeus: the Word of God is God's active instrument of creation. He creates everything with it.

Then, second: the word Irenaeus uses of the Holy Spirit is "wisdom" (Hebrew: *hokmah*; Greek: *sophia*). This also has an important active element about it for although it was thought of as an intellectual principle, wisdom was also fundamentally tied up with human life as it was lived in practice. And in Hebrew thinking, for example in the book of Proverbs, wisdom is personified as someone who was created by God before anything else, and was there with God from the very beginning helping him create and sustain the world (8:22–31). The early Christians very soon connected Jesus Christ with wisdom (1 Cor 1:24) and so connected Jesus with creation. In Genesis, of course, the Spirit (Hebrew: *ruach*) hovers over the water during creation (1:2). And this Spirit, already central to the Old and New Testaments and seen in Jewish thinking as a fundamentally active element in creation, is connected by Irenaeus to wisdom. For Irenaeus, the Logos and Wisdom are God's two hands, acting in creating and saving the world.

To think of the threefold nature of God as the Father and his two hands is a vivid way of reimagining what God is like. The image has obvious strengths: there's the expected "three in one" element. But hands are also creative. They move independently and together; they make and create things; and they're extremely personal. Hands are one medium through which we connect with the world. Through them we relate to other people, in shaking hands or in holding someone's hands. It is with our hands that we play an instrument, paint a picture or do the gardening. Hands are instruments of creative connection and feeling. We communicate with them and speak bodily through them. If we break an arm or sprain a wrist we will soon become aware how important our hands are. It makes good sense, therefore, to think of God's Word and Spirit as his two hands moulding, forming, and shaping creation. Like the potter with the clay (Jer 18:1–17). God uses his hands to take us and shape us into what he wants us to be. On Trinity Sunday and throughout the year, the two hands of God form a powerful image for our consideration of how God acts in the world and in our lives.

Bible Study Passages

Prov 8:22–31

Jer 18:1–17

John 1:1–18

Questions for Discussion

What do you make of the images of the Trinity mentioned above?

What, in your view, would be the best image for the Trinity?

Share your reactions to Irenaeus' image of the Trinity as God and his two hands.

How important is it for Christians to believe in God as a Trinity?

Think of a brand-new image for the triune God.

Further Reading

Fiddes, Paul S. *Participating in God: A Pastoral Doctrine of the Trinity*. London: DLT, 2000.

Rohr, Richard. *The Divine Dance: The Trinity and Your Transformation*. With Mike Morrell. New Kensington, PA: Whitaker, 2016.

PART 2

Living Faith

1

Jesus

CAESAREA PHILIPPI: JESUS THE TURNING POINT

CAESAREA PHILIPPI OR MODERN Banias is in the Golan Heights about an hour's drive northeast of the Sea of Galilee in the Holy Land. Israel occupied the area from Syria in 1967 and serious political tension now permeates the stunning beauty of the region. Not to be confused with Caesarea Maritima on the Mediterranean coast, this Caesarea nestles at about 1,150 feet above sea level on the southern slopes of the snow-capped Mount Hermon. Today, hundreds of skiers, walkers, and tourists enjoy the natural beauty of the surroundings. Important because of its water, Caesarea Philippi has had a religious focus from the earliest times. In the Old Testament, Hermon is a mountain held in high esteem (Ps 89:12). Some early Christians associated Hermon with the transfiguration of Jesus. And in the gospels, Caesarea Philippi is the place where Jesus asks his disciples the famous question, "Who do people say that I am?" For Christians today, the place and the question continue to present an opportunity for a dramatic turnaround in faith.

The region of Caesarea Philippi came into prominence in the second or third century BCE when a water shrine to the Greek god Pan was built there. Water poured out from a spring in a huge cave which was the focus of the shrine. Pan was the Greek dancing god of nature and fertility. Then, in 20 BCE the area fell under the control of Herod the Great, who built a temple to Emperor Augustus. When Herod died, his son Philip inherited the area and it became known as the place of the Caesar Philip or Caesarea Philippi. Here on this mountain the various gods of the world were acknowledged and worshipped: nature, politics, and power. Here, decisions about ultimate allegiance and commitment were made. It was already a place of decision-making long before Jesus arrived, so it's not surprising that his famous question is set here in the gospels.

The Caesarea Philippi narrative in the Synoptic Gospels (Matt 16:13–20; Mark 8:27–30; Luke 9:18–22) is usually thought to be a watershed or turning point. In Mark it comes at the center of the gospel constituting a moment of decision-making for the disciples. The incident is preceded by the healing of the blind man at Bethsaida (8:22–26) and followed by the transfiguration (9:2–8), three incidents all focusing on the nature of faith and the perception of who Jesus is. Mark locates the incident in "the villages of Caesarea Philippi" and Matthew has "the district of Caesarea Philippi." Luke doesn't mention the location at all and was perhaps unaware of its significance. Given the setting in Mark and Matthew Jesus is in effect asking: "Here among the various gods of the world, who do you say that I am?" The question doesn't arise in a vacuum or as a matter of religious preference. It's "which god among the many possible ones do you follow?" And this is about more than just having the right words in response; it's about commitment and turning your life around.

By way of response to Jesus' question, the disciples' answers include John the Baptist, Elijah or one of the prophets (v. 28). All these in their time asked for decisions and commitments (1 Kgs 18:20–46; Mark 1:4–8). They all stood up for things, spoke out and usually paid the price. Jesus makes the question more personal and direct: "But who do you say that I am?" It's then that Peter seems to hit the nail on the head: "You are the Messiah," he says. Peter "seems" to hit the nail on the head but when Jesus talks about suffering, he is dismayed and rebukes Jesus. And Jesus then rebukes Peter telling him he's really on Satan's side. Peter has the right words but doesn't realize what's involved. He knows Jesus is the "Messiah" but isn't ready for the practical consequences. Jesus then tells the disciples that they need to deny themselves, take up the cross, and follow him (Mark 8:34). They need to make a decision.

Jesus' journey to the cross is just beginning and it's now time for the disciples to see what following him really involves. No wonder Caesarea Philippi is the setting for the question. This is the most challenging context for their decision to be made. Jesus tells them that they can gain the whole world but still lose their lives (8:36). It's as if he's saying, "Your decision to follow me must be total. Is it me or these others? Where does your true allegiance lie? If you're ready to come with me and complete the journey, you'll need to see clearly what I'm all about." The question constitutes a turning point in the gospel narrative, in Jesus' own journey and mission, and in the disciples' lives.

Caesarea Philippi or Banias in the Holy Land is on many modern pilgrim itineraries. With its natural beauty, its vivid historical associations, and its contemporary political tensions, it reminds pilgrims of the many ideologies still pulling on hearts and minds today. The location still speaks of the same ancient challenge of nature, power, and politics competing for allegiance. Its history still confronts visitors with the same temptations to wealth, greed, and selfishness. And the place still questions the lifestyles of those who would follow Jesus. It is the perfect location to read the gospel narrative and to reconsider Jesus' message.

But wherever you are, it's the question that really matters: Will you make the decision to follow Jesus over against other possibilities? Will you give up everything to be with him? Will you walk with him in humility and selflessness along the way of the cross? Will you stay with him to the end? Will your faith only be a comfortable hobby or are you in it for real? The question Jesus put to his disciples at Caesarea Philippi still confronts his disciples today: who do you say he is? And your reply, whatever it is, will mark a dramatic turning point in your life as a disciple.

Bible Study Passages

Matt 16:13–20

Mark 8:27–30

Luke 9:18–22

Questions for Discussion

Discuss the most important "turning points" in your life.

What is the significance of Caesarea Philippi as the setting for Jesus' question to his disciples?

What answers do Jesus' disciples give to his question?

What are the differences between the three gospel accounts of this event and do they matter?

Why is this turning point still important today?

Part 2: Living Faith

Further Reading

Pritchard, John. *Living Faithfully: Following Christ in Everyday Life*. London: SPCK, 2013.

Woodward, James, et al. *Journeying with Mark*. London: SPCK, 2011.

THE SAMARITAN WOMAN: JESUS THE WATER OF LIFE

In the cloister garden of Chester Cathedral in the north of England a most striking sculpture can be seen. Cast in bronze and showing the figures of Jesus and the Samaritan woman from St. John's gospel, it is called the *Water of Life* and is the work of Stephen Broadbent. The two figures each form half a circle with the legs joining at the feet. Jesus is the lower figure while the woman seems to be coming to him. Their faces meet in an obvious moment of close encounter. There is circularity and movement in the piece along with sharp angles and tension. Jesus' hands cover the woman's as together they hold a bowl from which water constantly wells up. The water flows from the bowl onto a surface beneath and then down into the surrounding pond below. Traveling back up into the bowl inside the bronze, the water flows in a constant cycle. The whole piece is a "water sculpture" capturing something of the ambiguity and power of the gospel story. Broadbent's message is clear: Jesus provides the "water of life" constantly welling up.

The sculpture is based on the story in John 4:1–42, which also focuses on Jesus the water of life. Jesus passes through Samaria on his way from Judea to Galilee (vv. 3–4) and encounters a woman at a well. Jews had no dealings with Samaritans (v. 9; cf. Luke 10:25–37) and men and women didn't talk in public. The encounter is tense and dramatic. The well is on land bought by Jacob and given to his son Joseph (Gen 33:19; Josh 24:32). The woman has gone to get water. The conversation begins with Jesus asking the woman for a drink (v. 7) but as with all the stories in John's gospel the narrative operates on several levels at once and it turns out that Jesus himself is the drink she needs. She perceives that Jesus is a prophet and he points to the coming of the hour when all geographical division will be removed (vv. 19–24) and worship will be neither in Jerusalem nor on the Samaritan Mount Gerizim but "in spirit and truth" (v. 24). The living water, as opposed to the still well-water of the past, symbolizes a new relationship between God and his people.

Several themes in this dramatic story are noteworthy. First, Jesus breaks down a number of significant barriers. He is in Samaria, talking to a Samaritan and pointing to a time when racial and social differences will be insignificant. He shows that he is willing to enter a geographical and a theological landscape where many might have feared to tread. The crux is: "God is spirit, and those who worship him must worship in spirit and truth" (v. 24). The encounter also shows that gender barriers can be broken down as well. This is no abstract theologizing. The specific geographical location shows that Jesus is risking his own safety and reputation. His actions are a practical theology on the ground, showing a specific attitude to outsiders, and an example of what he really stands for: God's encompassing love for all people.

Then there's the theme of living water which symbolizes this state of affairs. In the Old Testament, water is a powerful symbol: the people of Israel pass through the Red Sea (Exod 14:21–31) and the river Jordan (Josh 3:7–17), and the water is symbolic of the formation of a new people. It also symbolizes thirst for God, as in Psalm 42:1, "As a deer longs for flowing streams, so my soul longs for you, O God. My soul thirsts for God, for the living God" (cf. 63:1; 143:6). In the New Testament and especially in John's gospel water is frequently a symbol indicating new life. It occurs often either as the setting or as a main theme of an event (John 1:19–34; 2:1–12; 3:1–21; 4:1–42; 5:1–14; 6:16–21; 7:37–39; 9:1–12; 13:1–20; 19:28; 19:34; 21:1–14). The encounter between Jesus and the Samaritan woman is the key water story in John's gospel.

And then there are the words "I am." When the woman says to Jesus that she knows the Messiah is coming, he replies, "I am he, the one who is speaking to you" (v. 26). These are the words summing up the name of God given to Moses in Exodus: "I AM WHO I AM" (3:14). They signify the presence of God himself. On a number of occasions in John's gospel, Jesus uses the words "I am" in relation to an image such as "the bread of life" (6:35), "the good shepherd" (10:14), or "the true vine" (15:1). In the case of the water of life, Jesus provides the water which wells up eternally.

Stephen Broadbent's sculpture at Chester Cathedral is a powerful physical retelling of the story of Jesus and the Samaritan woman. Both the image in bronze and the narrative in John's gospel tell of the life of God welling up from eternity. Jesus is the one whose life shows the life of God springing up. And it is his life that shows where real thirst can be satisfied. Water is the metaphor used for the life that comes from God through Jesus.

His life, death, and resurrection (his lifestyle and all that that involved) brings living water. And the content of the water metaphor is the bringing together of estranged people, communities, and genders, and the purifying of life and worship. This is also Paul's insight in Galatians when he says, "There is no longer Jew or Greek, there is no longer slave or free, there is no longer male and female; for all of you are one in Christ Jesus" (3:28). In John's gospel and in Broadbent's bronze, water is the physical stuff that symbolizes the real drink of God which is the unity of all people in spirit and truth. When we follow Jesus, we encounter the "water of life" which is the living water of God with which we never thirst. Broadbent's sculpture, like the story itself, captures something of the very well-springs of Christian faith.

Bible Study Passages

Ps 42

John 4:1–42

Gal 3:28

Questions for Discussion

Discuss some of the many different uses of water.

Why is water a particularly useful image for God?

What are the main themes of the account of Jesus meeting a Samaritan woman?

Which boundaries are broken down by Jesus in this story?

What other metaphors for God can you think of?

Further Reading

Bradley, Ian. *Water: A Spiritual History*. London: Bloomsbury, 2012.

Wright, Tom. *John for Everyone*. Part 1. Chs. 1–10. London: SPCK, 2002.

JESUS

STILLING THE STORM: JESUS AND THE CHAOS

One of Rembrandt's most famous works is *The Storm on the Sea of Galilee*, painted in 1633. It's his only painting of an event at sea and depicts Jesus and his disciples in a boat on the Sea of Galilee amid a great storm with water lashing in and the disciples struggling to survive. There are twelve disciples in the boat plus Jesus and Rembrandt himself. As the sea rises around them, they cling to the mast trying to avoid drowning. One of them even seems to be vomiting over the side of the boat. In the midst of all this, Jesus sits calmly, questioning their faith. In 1990, Rembrandt's famous painting became even more well known when it was stolen from its home in the Isabella Stewart Gardner Museum in Boston, Massachusetts. The theft was one of the greatest in United States art history and the canvas has never been recovered, though its frame still hangs in the museum. The painting depicts a dramatic gospel story which tells us that Jesus calms the storm if we have faith in him.

The gospel story of Jesus stilling the storm appears in all three Synoptic Gospels (Matt 8:23–27; Mark 4:35–41; Luke 8:22–25) but not in John. In Mark, it comes at the end of a chapter of Jesus teaching in parables. The words of Jesus have been paramount, now his deeds take over. The gospel story runs as follows: Jesus and his disciples are in a boat on the Sea of Galilee when a great storm arises. (Storms are typical on the Sea of Galilee where the wind blows down nearby valleys onto the sea.) Jesus is asleep at the stern and seems not to be bothered. This could easily symbolize his confidence in God (Ps 3:5; 4:8). The disciples panic and ask him why he's not concerned. He then stills the storm saying, "Peace! Be still!" (v. 39). The climax of the story is when Jesus asks, "Why are you afraid? Have you still no faith?" (v. 40). The Greek for "be still" has the sense of "muzzling" the chaos rather than eliminating it. The story is clearly about faith and discipleship but it has the deeper themes of creating and saving as well.

One of the most important things about this story is the setting on the sea. The Sea of Galilee is actually a freshwater lake but Mark calls it a sea, thus evoking a whole set of associations which are known in ancient Near Eastern literature. Most people understand the story simply as a miracle: Jesus breaks the laws of nature. But already in prebiblical traditions people understood the sea as a symbol of chaos and evil. A number of the ancient stories about creation involve a struggle in the sea, a struggle with chaos and demons. One of the most famous is the *Epic of Gilgamesh* in which

Part 2: Living Faith

Gilgamesh King of Uruk seeks eternal life after his friend Enkidu dies.[1] He goes to see Utnapishtim who tells him that in a dream he was commanded to build a boat and put every type of animal into it. During the raging of the sea the boat becomes the ark of salvation. By surviving the storm, Utnapishtim achieves eternal life. Other creation myths of the time include the destruction of sea monsters as part of the processes of creating and saving.

Stories like these have obvious parallels in the Old Testament. In Genesis 6–8 Noah experiences a flood and builds an ark of salvation which is part of God's way of dealing with chaos. The Psalms have God stilling the sea and defeating the dragons Leviathan, Rahab, and Behemoth. For example, "You rule the raging of the sea; when its waves rise, you still them. You crushed Rahab like a carcass" (Ps 89:9–10; cf. 33:7; 65:7; 74:13–14; 93:3–4; 107:23–32). And the sea is important at the end of time too. In the book of Daniel, the vision of the end-time includes the rising up of four beasts out of the sea (7:3) and one beast is destroyed (v. 11). In the vision of the new creation in the book of Revelation we learn that "the sea was no more" (21:1). In ancient Near Eastern literature and in the Old and New Testaments, calming the sea is the work of a God who defeats evil and creates the possibility of a new sort of world.

Rembrandt's famous painting of *The Storm on the Sea of Galilee* is a memorably vivid rendition of the gospel story, capturing the drama of the scene with great realism. Hopefully, one day it will be found and returned to its rightful home in Boston. The gospel story itself is richly woven with major theological themes which still speak to us today. The sea symbolizes creation in turmoil and chaos. Jesus is confident in God. And faith is what is needed to help create a different sort of world. In presenting Jesus as stilling a storm, the gospel writers show that he does the work of God, can eliminate chaos and evil, and bring order to creation. The message for disciples, then and now, is equally strong.

Throughout the gospels, the followers of Jesus are invited to join in his journey along the way of the cross and to take part in the work he does. In following Jesus and having trust in his ways, it is suggested, modern disciples can also play a part in the process of creating a calmer world and eliminating evil. In the many areas in which we struggle today—in politics, education, health care, environment, social care, and interfaith relations—we too can help defeat evil and bring order to creation by following Jesus. The Stilling of the Storm story reminds us of the place of Jesus and of our

---

1. See George, *Epic of Gilgamesh*.

own discipleship in creating a different sort of world, a world of calm harmony in which people are saved from the raging chaos.

Bible Study Passages

Ps 89:1–10

Ps 107:23–32

Mark 4:35–41

Questions for Discussion

In what ways does the sea symbolize chaos?

Discuss the idea that the sea symbolizes "pre-creation" chaos.

Discuss the different types of chaos you have experienced.

What is the main point of the Stilling of the Storm story?

In what ways can Jesus "still the storms" of the world today?

Further Reading

John, Jeffrey. *The Meaning in the Miracles*. London: Canterbury, 2001.

Newell, Edmund. *The Sacramental Sea: A Spiritual Voyage through Christian History*. London: DLT, 2019.

SPEAKING OUT: JESUS THE PROPHET

It's not very often we think of Jesus as a prophet but there are some real benefits in doing so. And there's an important sense in which Christians should think of themselves as prophets too. However, the word "prophet" has a number of associations that are quite misleading, so we must be careful.

At the mention of the word "prophet" you might think of Nostradamus the famous sixteenth-century astrologer who is said by some to have predicted many future events that have since occurred. It's been claimed that he foretold such things as the Fire of London, the rise of Adolph Hitler, and the September 11, 2001, attack on the Twin Towers in New York City. This popular perception that prophets are people who predict things sometimes hundreds of years ahead is widespread in popular culture today. And then you might think of the Prophet Muhammad. A very different figure, he is thought of more as the founder and leader of a religion, and the one to whom the Quran was dictated. But Jesus is hardly ever thought of as a prophet or called a prophet in Christian worship or discussion even though the New Testament clearly calls him such. In fact, for many, calling Jesus a prophet might seem something of an understatement. But there are important lessons to be learned from thinking of Jesus—and ourselves—as prophets.

If we're to think of Jesus as a prophet, it would be as one of the great prophets of ancient Israel. It's difficult to define them but we can point to a few important characteristics. The early prophets such as Elijah and Elisha seem to be inspired in the sense of ecstatic (1 Kgs 17—2 Kgs 13) and Jesus isn't quite like that. But they shared with the later prophets the urgent need to "speak out" against matters of social injustice. They usually had some sort of dramatic call (Isa 6:1–13; Jer 1:1–10; Amos 7:14–15) and then set out on a life of standing up for justice and true religion, usually against kings and queens or the wealthy in their own day. Jesus shares much more of this element.

The best known of the later Old Testament prophets are Isaiah, Jeremiah, Ezekiel, Hosea, Amos, and Micah. Their messages are critical of those who amass wealth and oppress the poor (Isa 10:1–4; Amos 6:4–8). They don't hold back in terms of "speaking out" against the prevailing regime. And they not only speak out, they also "act out" their messages within society in symbolic ways (Isa 20:1–6; Jer 19:1—20:6; and Ezek 4:1–17). Whatever else, it seems that the prophets of ancient Israel spoke out against injustices in their own day. They did not, on the whole, predict the future or speak about events hundreds of years ahead (though later writers often saw their utterances in that way). They were not like Nostradamus. More like Muhammad, perhaps. It's often said that the Old Testament prophets were "forthtellers" not "foretellers." They didn't predict, they pronounced. They addressed their contemporary situation and often compromised their own safety in doing so.

It's clear that Jesus was a prophet in this sense. The New Testament calls him a prophet and even though it says he was "more than a prophet" (Matt 11:9; Luke 7:26) he's certainly seen to stand in line with the Old Testament prophets. There are several general ways in which Jesus is presented as a prophet in the gospels. His simple lifestyle (Matt 8:20; Luke 9:58), his utterances ("Very truly, I tell you . . ." John 12:24), and the way he is presented as fulfilling prophecy himself (e.g., Matt 1:22–23; 8:17) are all indicators. Jesus has a prophetic-style call in his baptism (Mark 1:9–11), and his ministry is clearly one of both "speaking out" (Mark 1:15) and "acting out" the message of God's kingdom (Mark 4:35–41; John 2:1–11).

And then there are the more specific statements that Jesus is a prophet. The gospels of Matthew and Mark associate him with the prophets of ancient Israel (Matt 21:11; Mark 6:15; 8:28) but it's mostly in Luke and John that Jesus is called a prophet and there are some strong cases. In Luke, following the healing of the Widow of Nain's son, the people say of Jesus, "A great prophet has risen among us!" (7:16) and even after the resurrection on the road to Emmaus the theme of prophecy is brought in (24:19). In John's gospel Jesus is called a prophet by the woman of Samaria (4:19), after the feeding of the five thousand (6:14), in Jerusalem at the Feast of Tabernacles (7:40), and by the man born blind (9:17). But it's more than just being called a prophet. The gospel writers present Jesus as living a truly prophetic lifestyle. His words and deeds together contribute to his message and example. Not only does he "speak out," he also "acts out" the message. As disciples of Jesus, we can, in our own time and place, do the same.

Nostradamus, Muhammad, and Jesus were all different sorts of prophets. If we're going to think of Jesus as a prophet, then it's not as someone who predicted the future. Rather, he's someone who stood up for truth and justice among his own people. He stood up, spoke up, and acted out his message. And if Jesus is a prophet there's every sense that those who follow him should be like him. For the prophets of the Old Testament it was impossible to worship God and neglect your neighbor. And Jesus' message is the same (Matt 5–7; Luke 6:17–49). So, disciples of Jesus today should be prophets like him. We must stand up and speak out wherever the need arises and in whatever ways we can. We cannot love God and hate our neighbor (1 John 4:19–21). We cannot profess faith and ignore justice. And we cannot worship God without care of our neighbor. It may sometimes be costly to do it but we, like Jesus and the prophets, should always be trying, at least, to be truly "prophetic."

Bible Study Passages

Is 6:1–13

Luke 7:11–17

John 4:19

Part 2: Living Faith

Questions for Discussion

What do you think a prophet is?

What do the prophets of the Old Testament do?

What does it mean to call Jesus a prophet?

Share some of your experiences of prophecy.

In what ways can the church be prophetic?

Further Reading

Brueggemann, Walter. *The Prophetic Imagination*. Philadelphia: Fortress, 2001.

Hooker, Morna D. *The Signs of a Prophet: The Prophetic Actions of Jesus*. London: SCM, 1997.

PEOPLE AND PLACES: JESUS THE NEW TEMPLE

It's often said that people are more important than places. The people we live with, our families, neighbors, and the wider community are all more important than the place we live in. The people we go on holiday with are more important than where we go. The people in our church are more important than the building, and so on. And even though Christian faith is rooted historically in specific places, it's the person of Jesus Christ that lies at the heart of our faith. We may have had conversion experiences in particular locations or come to think of specific places as formative for our faith but in the end the person of Jesus is more significant. One illustration of this is the way the Jerusalem temple is interpreted in the New Testament. God is no longer associated primarily with a building, however sacred, but with a person. God no longer dwells in a house of stone but in a person: Jesus is now the new temple where God's presence can be encountered.

The Jerusalem temple lay at the center of ancient Judaism as the focus of Jewish life and thought. In layout and theology, it reflected the desert tent of meeting, tabernacle or sanctuary (Exod 25–40). The tent and especially the ark of the covenant carrying the tablets of the Ten Commandments signified the presence of God. The plan of the desert tent and ark was the basis of the temple built by King Solomon in Jerusalem, a glorious structure described in detail in the Old Testament (1 Kgs 6–7; 2 Chr 3–4).

This was essentially the "house of God," the place where God dwelt and where the divine presence was encountered by those making sacrifice. Solomon's temple was destroyed in about 586 BCE by the Babylonians when the Jewish people went into exile. Another temple was started in 536 when they returned and was then extended significantly by Herod the Great from 37 BCE onward. This rebuild, from 536 to the time of Herod, is usually known as the "second temple" and is the temple that Jesus knew. Throughout this entire period the Jerusalem temple was the focus of Jewish encounter with God.

The temple was divided into a number of different courts, each named after the group of people who could go no further into the complex. It was a series of graded zones leading up to the holy of holies where the divine presence itself dwelt. By far the largest area was known as the Court of the Gentiles. It was open to everyone, but the Gentiles could go no farther. Then, after the "dividing wall" (cf. Eph 2:14–16) came the Court of the Women. This was an area that Jewish men and women could enter but the women could go no farther. Next was the Court of the Israelites into which all male Jews could go. And then the Court of the Priests, followed by the Temple Court which was the specific area of sacrifice. Finally, the Holy of Holies lay behind a curtain. Here was the inner sanctum, the ultimate holy place, the house of God. In Solomon's temple it housed the ark of the covenant. In Herod's temple it was empty. Only the high priest was allowed to enter, and he only once a year on the Day of Atonement. Overall, the temple was a series of graded hierarchical zones leading up to the presence of God himself who was essentially distant and beyond immediate access, especially for ordinary people.

The early Christians took over much of the temple symbolism and used it in their thinking about Jesus. But now, of course, Jesus was more important than the temple. The person replaced the building. In the gospels, the temple appears frequently: Jesus challenges the temple (Matt 21:12–17; Mark 11:15–19; Luke 19:45–48; John 2:13–22); Luke's gospel begins in the temple (1:8–23); Jesus is taken there at his presentation (2:22–24) and when he is twelve years old (2:41–52); Jesus makes predictions about the temple (Matt 24:1–2; Mark 13:1–2; Luke 21:5–6); and, of course, the veil of the temple is torn in two at the time of his death (Matt 27:51; Mark 15:38; Luke 23:45). In the Epistle to the Hebrews, Jesus is the final priest and the final sacrifice of the temple (9:11–14). He is also said to be the veil or curtain of the temple (10:20). In the book of Revelation when the heavenly Jerusalem comes down from heaven there is no temple, "for its temple is the Lord God the Almighty and the Lamb" (21:22). Now, Jesus himself is the temple. He has become the location of the divine presence in the world. He has become the holy of holies and the sacred space of God's revelation. It is now in Jesus that God has his dwelling place, not in the temple. This most important idea is summed up when the fourth evangelist comments in his version of the Cleansing of the Temple story that the temple Jesus spoke about was his body (John 2:21).

People are more important than places. A person has taken the place of a building. Jesus has become more important than the Jerusalem temple. For Christians, the focus should always be on the person of Jesus and the life he lived rather than any place or text associated with him or any building erected in his memory. It is, rather, the example he set through the way he lived, his humility, compassion, and care for others that make him both the location where we find God's presence and the focus of our faith. For Christians today, it's not simply a fact that Jesus is the dwelling place of God instead of a building. It's the reason for this that matters: Jesus shows us something new about God and this makes him our "temple." It's here in a personal human life, lived out in a particular way, that we see God and find his presence in a special way. It's in a living person, not in a building, that God dwells. And for this reason, Christians can call Jesus the "new temple."

Bible Study Passages

1 Kgs 6:11–22

Mark 15:38

John 2:13–22

Questions for Discussion

What do you know about the Jerusalem temple?

What was the significance of the Jerusalem temple for the ancient Israelites?

In what ways is Jesus the "new temple"?

Share your experiences of finding God in a building.

Discuss the ways in which you have found God present in particular people.

Further Reading

Goldhill, Simon. *The Temple of Jerusalem*. Cambridge: Harvard University Press, 2005.

Perrin, Nicholas. *Jesus the Temple*. London: SPCK, 2010.

2

The Saints

MARY: SEAT OF WISDOM

MERTON COLLEGE, OXFORD, WAS founded in 1264 by Walter de Merton, Bishop of Rochester. In 2014 the college celebrated its 750th anniversary. Part of the celebration was the commissioning of a statue of the Virgin Mary and the child Jesus by the British sculptor Peter Eugene Ball. The statue sits in the south transept near the door of Merton chapel and has the title "Mary, Seat of Wisdom." Peter Ball's work can be seen in over sixty different churches and cathedrals across England including, for example, Chelmsford Cathedral (a Christ figure), Southwell Minster (a Christ figure), Blythburgh Church in Suffolk (a Madonna and Child), and Winchester Cathedral (a *Pietà*). Ball's work has become increasingly well known over the last half a century or so. It has a neo-Byzantine look about it and is deeply evocative and stirring.

The "Mary, Seat of Wisdom" statue is made of wood with Mary in blue, Jesus in red, and silver and gold copper covering some of the surface. It stands about four and a half feet high and is set on a plinth with a votive candle stand in front of it. Two large candles flank the statue. Mary is seated with Jesus on her knee. His right hand is extended in a gesture of invitation while his left hand is supported by her left hand as she holds him close to her. The faces speak of suffering, offering, and invitation. The statue has, at the same time, an ancient and a modern look about it, evoking a mysterious presence. What can we learn from this unusual piece of commemorative, devotional art?

Wisdom is something we don't hear much about these days at least in general life. Knowledge, skills, and even cleverness, perhaps, but we don't hear young people saying they want to be wise when they grow up. In the Old Testament, wisdom is very important and the "Wisdom Literature" (Job, Proverbs, and Ecclesiastes) consists of both narratives and sayings. More important is the concept itself. Ultimately, wisdom was thought of as part of God's very being, connected to his eternal purposes and his ways with the world. In Proverbs, wisdom is personified as a young woman who existed with God before the world was made and who helped in the processes of creation (8:22–31). In the first book of Kings, the famous King Solomon asks for wisdom and is given wealth as well (3:5–15). Solomon reigned in Jerusalem in the tenth century BCE. His fame spread far and wide and many, including the Queen of Sheba, traveled to hear his wisdom (1 Kgs 10:1–13). In Jerusalem, Solomon's ivory throne (1 Kgs 10:18–20) inevitably became known as the "seat of wisdom."

Later, Christian thought associated both Jesus and Mary with wisdom. In his First Letter to the Corinthians St. Paul says that Christ is the "power of God and the wisdom of God" (1:24). Paul contrasts the wisdom of the world with the wisdom of God. God's wisdom is characterized by humility and selflessness. Worldly wisdom is foolishness while God's foolishness is real wisdom (vv. 26–31). Mary was soon associated with wisdom too. In the second-century *Protevangelium of James* (an apocryphal gospel not in the New Testament), Mary is taken to the Jerusalem temple where she dances before God.[1] In Proverbs 8:30–31 it is wisdom that dances before God.[2] And in 2 Samuel 6:14 Solomon's father David dances before the ark of God after he has brought it to Jerusalem. But the reason why the early Christians saw Mary in terms of God's wisdom was primarily because of her response to God's call in the narrative of the Annunciation (Luke 1:26–38). Mary responds positively to Gabriel's message that God wants her to be the mother of the savior: "Here am I, the servant of the Lord; let it be with me according to your word" (v. 38). Mary says "yes to God" and allows herself to be drawn into God's purposes. Herein lies her wisdom.

Because of Mary's positive response to God, her willingness to do his will, and because of the incarnation of God in her body, Mary was often given titles and images from the Old Testament. She was thought of, for example, as the "ark of the covenant" and as the "burning bush." Just as

---

1. See Elliott, *Apocryphal New Testament*, 48–67. Mary dances before God on p. 60, par. 7.

2. "I was daily his delight" is usually interpreted to mean the child "wisdom" dancing before God.

God had been present in those places, so he was present in Mary who gave birth to the Word in Jesus. Mary was associated with wisdom and was thus described as the "Seat of Wisdom" which became an increasingly popular title for her in the Middle Ages. Looking at the statute in Merton College, Oxford, it's easy to see the line of thought: Jesus, who is God's wisdom, sits on the throne or seat of wisdom which is his mother. She is the seat upon which wisdom sits and is also wise herself.

What is the message of the image of "Mary, Seat of Wisdom" for us today? Focusing either on Mary herself as reflecting God's wisdom or on her giving birth to Jesus as God's wisdom allows us to consider our own response to God. How can we ourselves embody God's wisdom? How can we allow ourselves to be drawn into God's purposes for us? How can we let God act in us as both Jesus and Mary did? We can do this by saying "yes to God" wherever we find ourselves at any time and in any place, and also by following Jesus in his way of living out the "foolishness of God." It may be through a word of encouragement, a small act of kindness, a minor contribution to a good cause. Or, of course, in major acts of humility and compassion, in helping others, in prayer, teaching, and healing. In all of these ways we too, like Mary and Jesus, can embody God's wisdom, letting ourselves be drawn into his purposes and allowing his Word to be born in us. The idea of Mary as the "Seat of Wisdom" helps us refocus our own Christian lives and offers encouragement to us as we also try to do God's will and give birth to his wisdom in the world.

Bible Study Passages

1 Kgs 3:5–15

Luke 1:26–38

1 Cor 1:18–31

Questions for Discussion

What do you understand by the word "wisdom"?

Share experiences of people you think are wise.

In what ways was Mary wise?

What does it mean to say that Jesus was "God's wisdom"?

Where can wisdom be found today?

Further Reading

Pelikan, Jaroslav. *Mary through the Centuries: Her Place in the History of Culture*. New Haven: Yale University Press, 1996.

Warner, Marina. *Alone of All Her Sex: The Myth and Cult of the Virgin Mary*. London: Vintage, 2000.

THE CURÉ D'ARS: HUMILITY AND SIMPLICITY

On August 4, 1859, a famous French priest died in the village of Ars, twenty miles or so north of Lyons. About six-and-a-half thousand people attended the funeral. He was seventy-three years old and had become famous throughout the region for his priestly wisdom and spiritual direction. He had been parish priest of Ars for over four decades and had gained a reputation as an unusually holy man, one who in his humility and simplicity reflected God to the people around him and for whom he cared with an extraordinary depth of love and understanding.

In 1925 he was made a saint in the Roman Catholic Church, and after his death the small village where he had lived became a pilgrimage center. People flocked from far and wide to see the place where he had ministered. A new basilica was built where his body can still be seen in a glass case above the high altar. Today he is the patron saint of parish priests. His full name is John-Baptiste Marie Vianney although he is usually known simply as the "Curé d'Ars" meaning the priest of Ars. His feast day (in both Roman Catholic and Anglican Calendars) is August 4, the day of his death.

John Vianney was born in 1786 in Dardilly near Lyons. His family were simple farmers and John was one of six children. Soon after John's birth they were caught up in the French Revolution, and the Catholic Church was outlawed and replaced by the secular laws of the new regime. In order to practice their faith people held underground masses and said their prayers in private. John Vianney and his family became deserters, avoiding the authorities. John was soon confirmed by the local bishop and at the service of his first communion, covering had to be put over the windows of the church so that the candle light could not be seen from the outside. John wanted to become a priest but his education was already interrupted by the revolution and he was drafted into the army. On one occasion while staying on a farm, John hid in a haystack to avoid the police.

Part 2: Living Faith

John was physically weak but displayed a piety that eventually helped him get into seminary. He was not an able student and, in spite of his efforts, failed his exams. Eventually he was ordained deacon and priest because of his devotion and care for others. He was placed by the bishop in the small village of Ars, out of harm's way. But John's holiness soon became known far and wide and he was sought out for advice and spiritual direction. People came to him in the hundreds. It is said that John spent eighteen hours a day in the confessional and was overrun with the demands of his people. He led a starkly ascetic life and more than once ran away in search of monastic solitude. He joined the Third Order of St. Francis (TOSF) and lived a life of extreme humility and simplicity.

What was it that was so remarkable about John Vianney? He started in total insignificance and simplicity. He was not wealthy or prosperous. He had no worldly success or material possessions. But he became a saint. His life reflected God's life to the people around him. His way of life, like many of the saints, reflected the way in which God works through humility, simplicity, suffering, and failure to transform people to his purposes.

Not surprisingly, there are important connections between John Vianney and Jesus of Nazareth as he is portrayed in the gospels. Jesus is a man of humility and simplicity. He probably had little formal education. The gospels emphasize his care and love for others (e.g., Luke 10:25–37; John 11:5), his compassion, humility, and selflessness (Matt 5:38–48; Mark 10:35–45). Throughout the gospels there's an emphasis on Jesus the servant. At the Last Supper in Luke's gospel, Jesus himself says that he has come among the disciples as one who serves, not lording it over people like the kings of the Gentiles (22:24–27). In the Gospel of John, Jesus washes his disciples' feet (13:1–20) and his death on the cross is the supreme moment of his reflection of God's glory (19:30). St. Paul also clearly sees this aspect of Jesus when he speaks of him taking the form of a servant and suffering to death. Following this, God "highly exalted him" (Phil 2:6–11). In 1 Corinthians (1–2) Paul emphasizes the "foolishness of God" as God's real wisdom and power.

Perhaps the most important text summing up the truth found in the life of John Vianney and in the life of Jesus is 2 Corinthians 8:9, "For you know the generous act of our Lord Jesus Christ, that though he was rich, yet for your sakes he became poor, so that by his poverty you might become rich." Here Paul sums up the heart of his own theology in which the world as we usually think of it is turned upside down. God's richness is not like our richness. It is more like our poverty and weakness. God's richness and strength can be found in weakness and failure, and it is through poverty and simplicity that it can be experienced. In Jesus' servanthood and weakness, God's riches can be known.

The life of the Curé d'Ars reflects the same truth. In that small French village in the nineteenth century, John Vianney's life reflected God's life. His humility, simplicity, weakness, and failure reflected the way God works in the world. People saw God in this humble man and were attracted to him for that reason. God works with our weaknesses, failure, and humility, and transforms them into an opportunity for his own richness to be experienced. We can learn a lot from John Vianney today about the way God is with the world, transforming weakness and failure into the riches of his graceful purposes.

Bible Study Passages

Mark 10:34–45

Luke 10:25–37

Luke 22:24–27

Questions for Discussion

What do we know about the Curé d'Ars?

How important is it for ministers to be well educated?

What are the parallels between John Vianney and Jesus?

Discuss times when you have seen strength in weakness.

What do you understand by "the foolishness of God"?

Further Reading

Rutler, George William. *The Curé d'Ars Today: Saint John Vianney.* London: CTS, 2009.

Trochu, Abbé Francois. *The Curé d'Ars: St. Jean-Marie Baptiste Vianney.* Charlotte: Tann, 1992.

Part 2: Living Faith

ST. BENEDICT: PRAYER AND WORK

One summer, over forty years ago, I took off to France to the great Benedictine monastery of Solesmes in the region of Sablé-sur-Sarthe in the Loire Valley. The visit introduced me to the austerity and profundity of the Benedictine tradition, an experience that has stayed with me ever since. Solesmes is one of the biggest Benedictine houses in Europe, and I was struck by the powerful and formative combination of prayer and work in the daily life of the monks.

Originally founded in the eleventh century, Solesmes received a new burst of life in the nineteenth century under its famous Abbot Dom Prosper Guéranger. In the twentieth century, the Abbey played a key role in liturgical renewal, particularly in music. In the 1970s, at the time of my visit, Solesmes was widely known for its recordings of Gregorian chant. I already possessed several of the records and was well set up to appreciate the live performances when I got there. I attended the daily offices and Eucharist and started to absorb something of the Benedictine spirit which I continue to admire. I later learned that the famous French philosopher Simone Weil had stayed at Solesmes in Holy Week 1938 and how formative this had been for her faith.

Benedict was born in 480 in Nursia, Italy. Not much is known about his life but it seems that at the age of about twenty he went to Rome to study. Horrified by the wild life of the city, he decided to withdraw, giving up his studies and moving to a cave at Subiaco in Umbria where he stayed for three years. His cave was situated in a mountainous area below a monastery. The monks provided him with food and kept an eye on him. Soon, people were attracted to his contemplative lifestyle and gathered around him. He founded a series of twelve monasteries in the area but there was jealousy among the monks and Benedict himself decided to move to Monte Cassino between Rome and Naples where he founded the monastery that was to become his home and where he died in about 547.

It was while Benedict was at Monte Cassino that he wrote his famous *Rule* which focused on community life in a monastery. Influenced by some already existing monastic rules, Benedict's *Rule* was to become the basis of all Western monastic life and subsequent developments in monasticism for fifteen centuries until now. Its primary emphases are prayer and work, either manual labor or study. The Benedictine ideal based on the *Rule* is for community life based on eight hours of prayer a day in the round of monastic offices, eight hours of manual or other labor, and eight hours of sleep. When

The Saints

awake, the tasks are to pray and to work (*ora et labora*). The *Opus Dei* or "work of God" is prayer and work together. The combination is the distinctive feature of the Benedictines and prayer is sometimes seen as work.

Of course, the emphasis on prayer and work didn't begin with Benedict. They're both already there in the lives of Jesus and St. Paul. For Jesus, prayer is central. He withdraws for prayer on a number of occasions. It's a special theme in Luke's gospel where the setting of prayer is emphasized. When Jesus is baptized he is praying (Luke 3:21) and when choosing the disciples he "went out to the mountain to pray; and he spent the night in prayer to God. And when day came, he called his disciples and chose twelve of them" (6:12–13). He is at prayer at the time of the transfiguration (9:28–29) and prays in earnest in Gethsemane (22:39–46).

In the other gospels Jesus speaks with God on a number of occasions: for example, following the Raising of Lazarus (John 11:41–42), when he asked God to save him from his coming crucifixion in the "Johannine Gethsemane" (John 12:27–28), and of course in the longer High Priestly Prayer in John 17. He also teaches his disciples to pray with the Lord's Prayer (Matt 6:5–13; Luke 11:1–4). And he is found praying at the time of his crucifixion in all the gospels with his words from the cross: "My God, my God, why have you forsaken me?" (Matt 27:46; Mark 15:34); "Father, into your hands I commend my spirit" (Luke 23:46); and "It is finished" (John 19:30).

But it is also clear that Jesus works hard in preaching, teaching, and healing (e.g., Matt 5–7; Mark 1:15; Luke 14:1–6). And the disciples work hard too. They have given up their jobs but are still very active in the furtherance of the kingdom and in prayer (e.g., Acts 1:23–26; 4:23–31; cf. 7:54–60). And St. Paul also combines prayer and work in the service of God and Christ in his traveling and preaching (Rom 1:8–15; 1 Cor 1:4; 2 Cor 13:11–14). Unlike Benedict, Jesus, the disciples, and Paul are hardly monastic figures, but the combination of work and prayer is certainly noticeable in the literature about them.

My visit to Solesmes in France some forty years ago left a significant impression on me. The great monastery spoke of the ideal of prayer and work combined in a continuum in community life. In Benedictine houses across the world this combination is lived out on a daily basis. In England, the houses in Ampleforth, Downside, Worth, and West Malling (and others in the Anglican tradition) all follow the *Rule of Benedict*. They all remind us of the gospel values of prayer and work and that there is no sacred and secular but one life lived under God, one continuum in which everything comes from God and is given back to God. This combination or continuum not only provides a disciplined life for Christians, helping us realize that whatever we do is done for God and under God as his creatures, but also reflects and participates in God's own work in creation and re-creation. For God himself works in and through creation, bringing us into being and forming us. And in the stillness of our prayer he holds us in his own stillness, re-creating us, and bringing us to completion.

Bible Study Passages

Matt 6:5–13; Luke 11:1–4

Luke 6:12–13

Luke 14:1–6

Questions for Discussion

What do you know about St. Benedict?

Share your experiences of Benedictine communities.

What is so special about the combination of prayer and work?

Is there a distinction between the sacred and the secular and, if so, what is it?

What do Benedictine communities have to say to Christians today?

Further Reading

De Waal, Esther. *Seeking God: The Way of St. Benedict*. Norwich: Canterbury, 1999.

White, Carolinne, ed. *The Rule of Benedict*. London: Penguin, 2008.

ST. DOMINIC: PREACHING AND TEACHING

The Dominicans are a religious order that emphasizes preaching and teaching. You might have heard of *Blackfriars* in Oxford or the *École Biblique* in Jerusalem. They're both Dominican houses. The Dominican order stems from St. Dominic (1170–1221), a contemporary of St. Francis of Assisi (1181/2–1226). Dominic was born in Calaruega in Spain and was attracted to the religious life at an early age. Like Francis he lived in a period in which the Christian faith was often over-spiritualized, with creation and the material world getting neglected. Dominic saw the need for a more informed and active band of preachers, and so, founding houses at Prouille and Toulouse and traveling across Europe, he started a religious order that emphasized study, preaching, education, learning, spirituality, work in universities, and care for the poor. When the order later became known as the "Dominicans," it was noticed that the Latin *Domini Canes* means "Hounds of the Lord" or "Dogs of the Lord" so that became their nickname! The Dominicans are also known as the Order of Preachers and put OP after their names.

Why are preaching and teaching so important in Christian faith? Sometimes they've had bad press because of long and boring sermons or bad school teachers. But they're both crucial to our growth in faith. These days there's much more concentration on different methods of preaching and teaching than there once was, and there's no reason why sermons and classes should be bad experiences. But how should we think of preaching and teaching theologically?

First of all, preaching and teaching are clearly part of Jesus' own method of announcing God's kingdom. In the gospels, he preaches and teaches. We're told frequently that he gathered a crowd around him and spoke to them. This was often out in the open (Mark 4:1) although he may well also have expounded in synagogue gatherings in towns and villages as he did in Nazareth (Luke 4:14–30). When Jesus teaches in parables, he's also preaching his message of the kingdom of God (e.g., Matt 25; Mark 4; Luke 15). His first announcement in Mark's gospel is that the kingdom of God is at hand and he encourages his audiences to "repent, and believe in the good news" (1:15). In the Sermon on the Mount (Matt 5–7) and the similar Sermon on the Plain (Luke 6:17–49) there's clearly a lot of preaching and teaching together. In St. John's gospel there are huge blocks of teaching material, the so-called "discourses," which are also preaching (e.g., 6:26–59). There's no doubt that Jesus was a preacher and a teacher.

St. Paul also both preached and taught as can be seen from the account of his life and travels in Acts (e.g., 13:13–52; 17:16–34; 19:1–41) and from the mood and content of his own letters (e.g., Rom 5:12–21; 1 Cor 1:10–17; Phil 2:1–11). Without Paul's powerful preaching and teaching he would never have done what he did to spread the Christian faith across the Mediterranean world. His skills in setting up communities in places like Corinth and Philippi are evidence of his tremendous power as a preacher and teacher. His letters clearly include preaching and teaching together as he starts and builds up communities. Obviously, hundreds of disciples, saints, and ordinary Christians down the centuries have done enormous amounts of preaching and teaching.

Trying to define preaching and teaching, however, can be quite difficult. There are differences as well as overlaps. Teaching might be thought of more as providing information while preaching is aimed at trying to draw someone into a way of life or convince them of a particular view of something, but it's never clear-cut. In church life, both teaching and preaching involve persuading, convincing, and sharing the Word of God with the community, and this lies at the heart of the Christian understanding. Whenever there is a gathering for worship there is an opportunity for God's Word to be preached and taught. At most church services there are readings from the Old and New Testament usually including a psalm and a gospel reading. The sermon or homily then expounds or explains the readings and the learning curve might continue in later group discussions or Bible studies. In these ways, the Word of God is communicated to the people. In many churches this communication of the Word is balanced with the "sacrament" of the bread and wine of the Eucharist forming a twofold focus of Word and Sacrament. The Word or message of God is heard in Scripture and explanation alongside the sacrament of bread and wine. Of course, preaching and teaching are not found only in the sermon and explanation. There are important ways in which both can happen in different ways at different times, both inside and outside formal worship. In essence, both preaching and teaching in a Christian context are about bringing the reality of God to people, opening a space where God might become known more deeply.

For St. Dominic and the Dominicans, preaching and teaching are crucial to the ministry of the church. From the beginning, the movement wanted to see more education that would help people understand what the Christian faith is all about. They knew how important it is that the Word of God be preached well and heard by people. They knew that Scripture needed to be made accessible to people so that God's Word could be heard in the community. Above all, Dominic and the early Dominicans wanted to pin the Christian gospel back down into human experience, avoiding spiritualizing the message and divorcing it from life as it was generally understood, lived, and experienced. They knew that this could be done most successfully through education and learning. They saw the importance of bringing worship and understanding together through good preaching and teaching of the Word of God. The same is true today in an age in which preaching especially has a bad press. Indeed, there is a serious need today for accessible and effective preaching and teaching in all the churches. The Dominicans bear witness to this and set an inspiring example: perhaps we could all try to be "Hounds of the Lord" in preaching and teaching his Word.

Bible Study Passages

Matt 25:14–30

Luke 4:14–30

Acts 13:13–52

Questions for Discussion

Share your experiences of teaching and preaching.

In what ways are teaching and preaching both similar and different?

What have the Dominicans contributed to the church's teaching and preaching?

How did Jesus combine teaching and preaching?

What makes good teaching and preaching today?

Further Reading

Goergen, Donald J. *St. Dominic: The Story of a Preaching Friar*. Mahwah, NJ: Paulist, 2016.

Stevenson, Geoffrey, ed. *The Future of Preaching*. London: SCM, 2010.

ST. FRANCIS: THEOLOGY AND ECOLOGY

Quite early on in his time in office, Pope Francis started to change the way people look at things. The so-called "Francis effect" spread very quickly around the world in the early months of his papacy. He certainly took the Roman Catholic Church by surprise and especially the Vatican. A new day was dawning and the new pope saw new opportunities. As leader of the world's one billion Roman Catholics and the most prominent leader of Christians in the West, Francis has a powerful religious and political role and can influence life at both global and local levels. He is the first pope from the Third World, the first Jesuit pope and the first pope to call himself Francis after the great medieval Saint Francis of Assisi (1181/2–1226). Indeed, much of what Pope Francis has to say is rooted in the theology of his famous namesake of Assisi.

One of the ways in which popes communicate is through circular letters called "encyclicals." The papal encyclicals carry considerable weight because of the status of the Bishop of Rome or the pope in the Roman Catholic Church. Encyclicals are official teaching. Since being elected to the job in March 2013, Pope Francis has issued two encyclicals: *Lumen Fidei* (The Light of Faith, 2013) and *Laudato Si'* (To You Be Praise, 2015). Encyclicals are always known by their Latin titles which are taken from the opening words of the text. The recent *Laudato Si'* has become particularly well known because it's about the environment, climate change, ecology, and the Christian faith. Its subtitle is "On Care for Our Common Home." Causing not a little controversy because the subject has huge political ramifications, the pope draws attention to the need to respect the whole of creation. What exactly does he say?

Laudato Si' opens with reference to the *Canticle of the Sun*, by St. Francis of Assisi, which refers to Brother Sun and Sister Moon, evoking a strong sense of the personal in nature. The pope follows St. Francis's love of creation and develops this into a reading of the contemporary environmental crisis. He draws attention to the deterioration of the earth through climate change, global warming, the disappearance of species, human exploitation of the earth, and the destruction of the ecosystem. He connects this deterioration to the amazing development of technology in the last century which, in spite of the progress it has enabled, he says, has brought with it an objectifying and manipulative attitude toward nature.

The pope connects this attitude with the consumerist outlook which sees everything in terms of its usefulness to human beings. This, he says, is breeding a paradigm that is taking over the entire global community, encouraging selfishness and individualism. For Francis, our contemporary culture in the West is throwaway, shallow, and destructive, based on the desire for instant gratification. And contrary to popular perception, this outlook isn't neutral. It brings with it a demise of values and respect for nature and people, and ends up neglecting important social issues in society, especially the needs of the poor. By way of beginning to counter this cultural paradigm, Pope Francis emphasizes that everything is connected and that attitudes in one area affect attitudes in another. We need to recover an awareness of our personal relation to the earth and to God our creator.

The pope's view of the earth is, of course, rooted in ideas and experiences of God as creator. In Genesis, God sees the creation as "very good" (1:31). The pope follows the now popular line on interpreting Genesis: human beings are in a position of stewardship rather than domination. We should look after the earth, not subdue and destroy it. At the present time we should recognize that the earth is in a state of crisis and begin to respond. And so, we need a more holistic way of living, a change of lifestyle that will start to heal the earth. This concern for the earth sees ecology, politics, economics, social concern, religion, and work as all related to each other. The pope encourages a change of attitude, based on a concern for the common good. An approach which sees the earth and other people as valuable can form the basis of dialogue and respect, he says. The earth which is our home and God's home, can only be healed if we live with humility and restraint. Such a lifestyle would recover a sense of our personal relation to creation and to God who is known partly in and through creation.

Pope Francis has gained a great deal of popularity in his time as pope and his encyclical *Laudato Si'* came at a significant moment. It points us toward something we desperately need to take into account in our common Christian thinking at this time: there's a substantial connection between God and creation. Our beliefs about God are connected to our beliefs about creation, nature or the earth. And our ways of living in the world reflect our basic attitudes. These may be subconscious and we may not even know they're there, but they often determine the way we see God and the world, and the relation between them. It's interesting that the early Christians took from Judaism a strong sense of God as a creator whose power and life can be seen in creation (Gen 1–2; Ps 19:1). They also connected their experience of Christ with God's creative powers (Prov 8:22–36; John 1:3; Col 1:15–20). Down the ages, Christians have affirmed their belief in God as creator in the words of the Apostles' and Nicene Creeds: "maker of heaven and earth."[3]

But today it often feels as though God's presence in creation is forgotten, even by Christian believers, and the world of nature is of no concern. Often, neglect of the earth sits alongside otherwise quite strong Christian belief and practice as if there's no connection. Following St. Francis of Assisi, Pope Francis's encyclical reminds us that our attitudes to nature and to

---

3. See, e.g., *Common Worship*, 77 and 173.

God are deeply connected and that if we care for creation more seriously and more personally, we shall come to a more complete awareness and experience of God.

Bible Study Passages

Gen 1:31

John 1:3

Col 1:15–20

Questions for Discussion

In what ways do you think of the earth as your "home"?

What does it mean to claim that God is "creator" of the world?

Why did some New Testament writers connect Christ with creation?

What is wrong with seeing the world as objective and ourselves as individuals?

Discuss the things we can do to care for the earth.

Further Reading

Cunningham, Lawrence S. *Francis of Assisi: Performing the Gospel Life*. Grand Rapids: Eerdmans, 2004.

Pope Francis. *Laudato Si': On Care for Our Common Home*. London: St. Paul's, 2015.

3

Christian Faith

CHELEY PARK: GOD IN NATURE

High up in the mountains (nearly eight-and-a-half thousand feet) seventy-five miles northwest of Denver, Colorado, USA, just near Estes Park, lies Cheley Camp, the home of the famous Cheley Colorado Summer Camps started in 1921 by Frank Cheley and his wife, Eva. Close to the Rocky Mountains, Cheley consists of roughly thirteen thousand acres of stunning parkland where the Cheley family have worked with teenagers for four generations. The aim of the Cheley Camps is to offer young people the opportunity to spend time exposed to nature, to live together for a month or so in the summer getting to know the environment and learning something of life outdoors, and living together. The aim is to help form Christian character and to assist in bringing participants to know their dependence upon and relation to nature in the context of community activity. Frank Cheley's vision was originally born out of his work with the YMCA during the First World War. To this day his influence survives in the hearts of all those who have been to summer camp at Cheley.[1]

Frank Cheley was an inspired leader and an engaging storyteller. He wrote a number of books including his well-known *Letters from God*, talks given in Cheley Camp's Hillside Chapel during the last years before he died. In the book, he articulates in simple language his understanding of the evidence for God in nature. Spending a month living close to nature for Cheley not only revealed something of the beauty of nature but also something of

---

1. Cheley Camp holds its centenary celebrations in 2020, marking the hundred years since preparations began.

its inner workings and this bore upon his understanding of God's relation to the world. To observe nature at close range, for Cheley, was to observe growth, development, and change. He saw the exquisite color of the trees as they came into blossom, the movement of the seasons and the beauty of the Rocky Mountains close by. He saw the promise of nature as things grew and died. And he saw the natural burst of life which would not be stunted or repressed. He was aware of the struggle of creation as it grew toward completion. And above all, he saw the connections between the promise of nature and the promise of the young lives of those taking part in his camps. He saw the value of courage and determination, of energy and participation. The inscription in wood at the Cheley Camp Hillside Chapel is the beginning of Psalm 121: "I will lift up mine eyes unto the hills . . ." (KJV).

Human beings have experienced God in nature from the earliest times and the Bible is full of it. God is the creator of the physical world and leaves his stamp upon what he makes. He is the author of creation and his hand can be seen at work in it. The book of Genesis (1–11) outlines the biblical story of creation and portrays God working in and through creation as he builds up its many and various layers. In Genesis there are two accounts of creation (chs. 1 and 2) but basically God creates the physical universe, human beings, and animals and then "recreates" following the fall of Adam and the destruction brought by the flood (chs. 3–11). The same strong sense of the creator God comes through in the book of Isaiah where God's creative action is portrayed in vivid poetry: "Who has measured the waters in the hollow of his hand . . . ?" (40:12). The notion of God the creator also permeates the Wisdom Literature of the Old Testament (Job, Proverbs, and Ecclesiastes) where Wisdom itself is God's instrument of creation: "The Lord created me at the beginning of his work . . ." (Prov 8:22) and, "When he established the heavens, I was there . . ." (v. 27). The idea that creation reflects God's own nature as the work of the artist reflects the character of the artist is especially vivid in Psalm 19:1, "The heavens are telling the glory of God; and the firmament proclaims his handiwork." No wonder Joseph Haydn set these words to music in his glorious oratorio of 1797/8, *The Creation*.[2]

It is striking that Christianity also sees the energy and power of God in creation. From the earliest times, Jesus was connected to creation in the minds of Christians. He is portrayed in St. John's gospel as the Logos, the instrument of all creation (John 1:1–3). And St. Paul sees him as "the

---

2. For an excellent recording, see Gardiner, *Creation*.

firstborn of all creation" (Col 1:15) and as the basis of the new creation (2 Cor 5:17; Gal 6:15; Col 3:10). The book of Revelation brings the whole biblical message of God and creation to a climax in its vision of a new heaven and a new earth at the end of time. It is focused on Jesus the lamb who is the basis of the new creation (Rev 21). From Genesis to Revelation there's a sense of the movement of God in creation and in Christ as God's purposes are worked out in the physical world. And the Christian Creed, recited regularly in worship, professes belief in God as creator: "We believe in one God . . . maker of heaven and earth, of all that is, seen and unseen."[3]

Frank Cheley's vision of God in creation led to him establishing influential annual summer camps in the beautiful mountains of Colorado in the 1920s. Cheley was aware not only of the energy and growth of creation itself but also of the revelation and unfolding of God's own life in nature. His vision of camps for young people was based on the observation that they grow and develop just as nature grows and develops, and he knew that the various signs of blossoming and unfolding in nature and in the lives of human beings were part and parcel of God's own life unfolding in the creation which he is constantly making and remaking. Cheley's sense of the revelation of God in creation was the basis of everything he did. That same sense of God breathing through creation has lain at the heart of Christian experience and faith throughout the centuries. Cheley saw God's hand or "Letters" in the movement of nature. His vision inspires us to see the same thing today.

Bible Study Passages

Ps 19

Ps 121

Col 1:15–20

Questions for Discussion

Where have you seen "letters from God" in nature?

Where do you find God especially present?

Are there places where you think God is absent?

What does it mean to say that Christ can be experienced in creation?

---

3. See, e.g., *Common Worship*, 173.

Part 2: Living Faith

What can we learn from nature about our own growth and development?

Further Reading

Cheley, Frank H. *Letters from God*. Whitefish, MT: Literary Licensing, 2011.

Ward, Keith. *The Evidence for God: The Case for the Existence of the Spiritual Dimension*. London: DLT, 2014.

FOOD AND DRINK: METAPHORS OF DIVINE LIFE

Food. What's your favorite? Indian perhaps? A good Biryani or Balti? A curry or korma? Papadums? And what about the temperature? Mild, medium, or hot? Take away or sit down? It makes no matter. Or perhaps you go for Chinese? Bamboo shoots and king prawns? Sweet and sour chicken? Rice or noodles? Any prawn crackers? Or maybe Italian? A good spaghetti, lasagne, or pizza? Or perhaps the English way: fish and chips, mushy peas, and a pickled onion? The possibilities are mouth-watering. Are you veggie or a carnivore? And what do you drink with your favorite food? A good house red or white? Merlot, Frascati, or Rioja? Or maybe soft: orange juice or elderflower? A cup of coffee or a glass of water? They all wash it down! Food and drink, how they feed and nourish us. How they seep through our bodies permeating every fiber. How we are what we eat. And without bread and water at least, we die.

There has always been a connection between religion and eating and drinking. There's the actual practice of eating and drinking during worship and then there's the use of food and drink as metaphors in religious texts. In many ancient religions, food was a part of religious worship. Sacrificing an animal and eating its flesh were central to a number of different traditions. St. Paul certainly knew of this as he dealt in his First Letter to the Corinthians with issues relating to food that had been sacrificed to idols in local temples (chs. 8 and 10). In Judaism, dietary laws were part of the requirements of the religion and the concept of *kosher* food still forms a part of that faith. For the early Christians the question of whether Jewish and other food laws still applied soon became a central concern. In Islam, similar food laws are known as *halal*.

In the New Testament, Jesus eats and drinks quite often. His critics say of him that he eats with sinners and tax collectors (Mark 2:15–17). He is no ascetic like John the Baptist (Mark 1:4–8). He's a dinner party man, out at meals with friends and outcast alike. He invites all sorts of people to the table and shares food with them. And even when food is not the subject of concern in a particular gospel story, the setting might easily be a meal (Luke 7:36–50). In general, we can think of Jesus feeding the four thousand (Matt 15:32–39; Mark 8:1–10) and the five thousand (Matt 14:15–21; Mark 6:35–44; Luke 9:10–17), and eating and drinking at the Last Supper (Matt 26:26–29; Mark 14:22–25; Luke 22:14–23; 1 Cor 11:23–26). And on many other occasions too there is mention in the gospels of grain, bread, water, wine, and fish (e.g., Mark 2:23–28; 4:2–9; 4:26–29;12:1–12; Luke 24:30, 42–43; John 15:1–11). Food and drink are clearly important in Jesus' day-to-day life at the physical and social levels.

And then there's the metaphorical sense. This is especially noticeable in St. John's gospel where eating and drinking crop up quite a bit and where they clearly have metaphorical as well as literal meanings. Some key events in John come easily to mind here. At the wedding in Cana of Galilee, water and wine are central (2:1–11). When Jesus meets the Samaritan woman at the well the subject is water and the dialogue moves toward Jesus himself as the real water (4:1–42). Jesus feeds the five thousand (6:5–14) and is himself the bread of life (vv. 35–59). He attends a meal in the house of Lazarus in Bethany (12:1–8) which is soon followed by the Last Supper (13:2–20) at which, curiously, there is neither bread nor wine. Their significance appears elsewhere in the Bread of Life discourse in chapter 6 and the Vine discourse in chapter 15. In the Passion Narrative, Jesus uses the metaphor of drinking to refer to his suffering (18:11) and on the cross he is thirsty (19:28–30). One of the resurrection appearance stories in this gospel occurs in the context of a breakfast of fish and bread (21:9–14). In John's gospel, food and drink are metaphors for God feeding and nourishing his people through Jesus.

Metaphors work by speaking of one thing in terms of another or saying that one thing is another. A metaphor is an image that helps us to see more deeply into the meaning of something. We use metaphors all the time without even noticing. Most sentences ever uttered or written contain metaphors. The "arm" of a chair, for example, is a metaphor using part of the human body for part of a chair. Defeating someone's arguments uses a war metaphor for a discussion. The Bible uses metaphors frequently, for example when it calls God a king (Ps 97:1) or a rock (Ps 18:2) and when it calls Jesus a lamb (John 1:36) or a vine (John 15:1). Talking about God and Jesus are complex matters and it's not surprising that people use metaphors to help. They are doors or windows into deeper levels of perception and understanding.

Indian, Chinese, Italian, English. Or just our basic daily food and drink. It's all enjoyable stuff for those who have it. And it is crucial to life and health in that it nourishes our bodies and sustains us. When food and drink are used in biblical texts such as the feeding of the five thousand or the woman at the well, they are metaphors for the real feeding that God gives to those who follow him. One thing stands for another, and food and drink are metaphors for the way God's life seeps into our lives and for the way in which our lives are bound up with his life and are dependent upon it. Food and drink are metaphors for the feeding that God gives us through nourishing us at every level. Whatever physical food and drink we might prefer and whatever metaphors might be used, the most important thing is this: God himself is our real life, health, and nourishment; he is our ultimate food and drink.

Bible Study Passages

Mark 6:35–44

John 2:1–11

1 Cor 10:23–33

Questions for Discussion

What sort of food do you enjoy most?

Why are eating and drinking so important in religion?

What are the most important gospel passages about eating and drinking?

How do metaphors work and why are they important?

What other metaphors are there for the way God feeds us?

Further Reading

Lakoff, George, and Mark Johnson. *Metaphors We Live By*. Chicago: University of Chicago Press, 2003.

Wirzba, Norman. *Food and Faith: A Theology of Eating*. Cambridge: Cambridge University Press, 2011.

Christian Faith

PERSONAL MARK: A SENSE OF MYSTERY

Back in 1977, the well-known actor Alec McCowen learned by heart the whole of St. Mark's gospel in the King James Version. He achieved great success on stage in the UK and North America reciting it solo with only a chair and table, a glass of water, and a small copy of the New Testament with him. The performance astonished everyone who heard it and inspired many to look through a completely new lens at the first gospel ever written. McCowen was already well known for his parts in *Hadrian VII* and *Equus* among other things, but performing a gospel in an old version of English was completely unexpected. He started his performances of *St. Mark's Gospel* in Newcastle and then took the show to the London Mermaid and Globe theaters, then to New York to Broadway, and to a few other American cities. After several years' performance followed by several years' break, he did it all again in the 1990s to similar acclaim. Others have done the same with other gospels but McCowen's performance is now considered a classic.

To experience McCowen's *St. Mark's Gospel* and to hear the ancient story about Jesus in a single sitting was truly inspirational. The new context took the gospel out of the church, for a start, and made it available to hundreds of non-churchgoers. It was alive, fresh, immediate, and dramatic in its fast-moving series of narrative events. The performance drew people into the story like a play and made them feel part of what was happening. And one of the main things was that people heard the gospel as a whole. This was unusual. In church, people only hear portions appointed for a particular day. No one hears the whole thing and few ever sit down to read it in its entirety. But it is quite likely that people would have originally heard the gospel read out as a whole, perhaps in a gathering for worship. To hear McCowen recite it all at once (one short interval and ice cream after 9:1!) brought something about this gospel out into the open: it has main themes and an overall mood and message.

The message is of the kingdom of God and Jesus' teaching about it in word and deed. There are parables and miracles, encounters and healings, and a substantial account of the final days leading to Jesus' death. The message of the cross hangs over the entire gospel and though there is an empty tomb story there are no resurrection appearances. But another element comes over even more clearly when the gospel is heard whole: an element of enigma and uncertainty, a sense of movement back and forth between knowing and not knowing.

Part 2: Living Faith

There are several pointers to this aspect of the gospel. First, it has a surprising opening (1:9) when Jesus suddenly appears as an adult from "Nazareth of Galilee." There are no birth stories as in Matthew and Luke and no reference to Bethlehem. Then there's something strange about the way the parables seem to be designed to prevent people from understanding (4:10–12). There's a combined theme of secrecy and revelation, the so-called "Messianic Secret": on some occasions when Jesus has performed a healing he tells people not to tell anyone (3:12; 5:43; 8:30) and on other occasions everyone seems to know (5:20; 7:36). There might be a gradual sense of Jesus' identity being revealed here, but it looks more like a kind of portrayal of the mysteriousness of Jesus and of God: things are moving, not a hundred percent clear, there's paradox and mystery. There's also the fact that in this gospel the disciples never seem to grasp what's going on (4:41; 6:6; 6:52; 8:21; 9:10; 9:32). They are part of Jesus' inner group and yet they seem to be in a fog about what it's really all about. Throughout the gospel, all these elements slowly create an effect of mystery and uncertainty.

The final example of this mysteriousness is the ending of the gospel when the women visit the tomb. They went away and "said nothing to anyone, for they were afraid" (16:8). Even though the tomb is empty and the resurrection has happened, there's still a sense of silence, uncertainty, and fear. And all this gives the impression that for this gospel writer the experience of God, the business of following Jesus, and the life of faith do not provide "all the answers." Things do not come in clear, tidy packages. In fact, following Jesus brings uncertainty and confusion, a sense of entering the "hiddenness of God" more than attainting total clarity. Faith can be a confusing challenge, this gospel seems to be saying, and though it is a life-changing experience of the living God and the risen Christ, it often leads us into less clarity rather than more. This important element in Christian faith was to become central in later centuries.

Alec McCowen's one-man solo stage performance of *St. Mark's Gospel* attracted hundreds of people. And they went back again and again. Even the ones who thought they knew the text well and heard it read out regularly in church noticed new things about it. McCowen wrote up his understanding of the gospel in his book *Personal Mark*. It shows that this gospel has a particular theological message wrapped up in its literary design. Main themes and overall patterns emerge and can only really be appreciated by hearing it whole. Mark's message is one of the mysteriousness of the Christian faith, of the uncertainties of Christian life, and of the hiddenness of God. The other gospel writers iron out some of these rough edges and put in clearer parameters. But Mark, thank goodness, preserves the profound insight that sometimes we might need to know less before we can know more, and that knowing the unknowable God and following Jesus might leave us more uncertain than certain. Thanks to St. Mark for inviting us into a profound vision of Christian faith and life, and to Alec McCowen for reminding us of Mark's message.[4]

Bible Study Passages

Mark 3:1–12

Mark 4:10–12

Mark 6:45–52

Questions for Discussion

Read St. Mark's gospel straight through. What are your impressions?

What are the signs of mystery and uncertainty in this gospel?

Why does Jesus want to conceal his identity on some occasions?

In what ways does your faith make you less certain about things?

What does it mean to say that God is a mystery?

Further Reading

McCowen, Alec. *Personal Mark*. London: Hamilton, 1984.

Williams, Rowan. *Meeting God in Mark*. London: SPCK, 2014.

BACH AND THE MUSTARD SEED: THE PROMISE OF THE KINGDOM

When I was a teenager in the 1970s learning to play the organ in Nottingham, I soon discovered the works of Johann Sebastian Bach. Of course, the beginner's staple was the *Eight Short Preludes and Fugues* but I also started buying recordings of some of the more complicated works. In those

---

4. For a fascinating movie rendition of Mark's gospel, see Batty, *Gospel of Mark*. This is part of the Lumo Project for which the other three gospels have also been done. See www.lumoproject.com.

PART 2: LIVING FAITH

days the 33 rpm vinyl records (now popular again) produced some of the best sounds and I found a recording by a well-known organist, still alive, called Lionel Rogg playing the then quite new Metzler and Son organ in the Grossmünster in Zurich. One track on the record was Bach's famous *Passacaglia and Fugue* in C minor (BWV 582).[5] It struck me as a staggering piece and I listened to it again and again.[6]

The piece begins with a very simple tune, actually written by a well-known French organist of Bach's own day, André Raison. Bach takes this theme and uses it as the basis of his own composition. He begins by stating the simple tune and then builds it up, layer upon layer through into the fugue which itself starts from another simple statement of the same tune. As the theme develops and the layers are added, the music turns into one of the most magnificent pieces ever written for the "King of Instruments." Not only does something enormous grow out of extremely small beginnings but from the beginning there is a strong sense of the promise of things to come.

This concept of the promise of growth from small beginnings reminds Christians of at least one of Jesus' parables in the New Testament: the Mustard Seed (Matt 13:31–32; Mark 4:30–32; Luke 13:18–19). Here the smallest seed grows into something enormous. And the promise is already contained in the seed. The parables of Jesus are essentially "comparisons" or "illustrations," something "thrown alongside" something else (Greek: *para*, alongside; and *ballo*, I throw) in order to bring out the meaning or reveal a deeper level. They are metaphors, symbols, images, and even allegories that enable something otherwise unclear to become clearer. Jesus' parables are known as "parables of the kingdom" because they're designed to illustrate what the kingdom of God or kingdom of heaven is like. Some of the best-known gospel parables are the Good Samaritan (Luke 10:25–37), the Prodigal Son (Luke 15:11–32) the Lost Sheep and Lost Coin (Matt 18:12–14; Luke 15:3–10), the Wise and Foolish Virgins, and the Sheep and the Goats (Matt 25:1–13; and 31–46). But the ones that come quickly to mind when hearing Bach's music are the "parables of growth," that is the Sower (Matt 13:3–23; Mark 4:1–20; Luke 8:4–15), the Mustard Seed (as above), the Seed Growing Secretly (Mark 4:26–29), the Tares (Matt 13:24–30), and the Dragnet (Matt 13:47–50).

---

5. BWV = *Bach-Werke-Verzeichnis*, indicating the system of cataloguing Bach's works.

6. A superb rendering on CD is Hurford, *Bach*.

In some respects, all Jesus' parables are about growth but these agricultural illustrations show in a particularly vivid way how growth in the earth is like growth in the kingdom. The Mustard Seed and the Seed Growing Secretly illustrate different but related aspects of this. The parable of the Mustard Seed occurs in the three Synoptic Gospels as well as in the *Gospel of Thomas*.[7] The seed is presented as the smallest seed, probably the black mustard grown in Palestine in gardens and fields. It can be used ground in oil and spice. It isn't actually the smallest seed, but the point is the same: something enormous comes from something really small, and the seed contains the promise of what will emerge later. The mustard grows quickly, so the emphasis is on small beginnings and impressive endings rather than on slow growth.

The parable of the Seed Growing Secretly brings out an element of hidden beginnings. Sometimes God's reign can begin in quiet, unknown places, only to grow into something very much larger later on. It doesn't matter whether we think of the seed growing in an individual person, in a community, in creation or in God's people. The point is the same: that God's hidden growth develops into something spectacular later. The promise is there even where the growth cannot be seen. And when harvest comes, the scythe is put in and there is great produce.

J. S. Bach's magnificent *Passacaglia and Fugue* in C minor grows from a simple germ stated in the first few bars into something quite majestic. The "Passacaglia" is a straightforward theme and the fugue is also a simple tune. They both grow from something small into a many-layered and richly-textured piece of music. A similar musical form is the "theme and variations" in which a simple theme grows into many different versions. Bach's *Passacaglia and Fugue* in C minor is itself a parable of the kingdom of God: as with the music, so with the kingdom. Jesus' parable of the Mustard Seed illustrates the same reality. The promise of God's kingdom is already there in the seed. And it's not just a matter of small things growing into something bigger. The promise of the kingdom of God is already wrapped up in the small seed. This is what the kingdom is like: it doesn't necessarily begin as something huge and successful in worldly terms. There's an inner growth from the barest beginnings and the final outcome is already there at the beginning.

---

7. See Elliott, *Apocryphal New Testament*, 123–47. The parable of the mustard seed appears on p. 138, para. 20.

And all this translates into the way in which the kingdom of God grows in our own day, in our churches and communities, in our societies and countries, and in the world at large. The small things we do and the insignificant beginnings we make are often accompanied by a sense that nothing is happening as a result of our efforts. But the small seeds we sow, like Bach's music, contain the promise of the kingdom. Whether it be in personal relationships and dealings with others, in matters in church and community life or in political matters on a national or global scale, small beginnings can grow into majestic achievements. We should not hesitate to sow the small seeds, for it is in them that the promise of the kingdom is contained. From small beginnings, as in Bach and the Mustard Seed, spectacular things can emerge.

Bible Study Passages

Mark 4:1–20

Mark 4:30–32

Matt 13:24–30

Questions for Discussion

Which pieces of music show growth from small beginnings?

Discuss the "parables of growth" in the gospels.

Give examples of growth from small beginnings in your church and community.

What do we mean when we say something has "promise"?

What sort of growth should Christians look for?

Further Reading

Blomberg, Craig L. *Preaching the Parables: From Responsible Interpretation to Powerful Proclamation.* Grand Rapids: Baker, 2004.

Levine, Amy-Jill. *Short Stories by Jesus: The Enigmatic Parables of a Controversial Rabbi.* New York: HarperCollins, 2015.

CHRISTIAN FAITH

C. S. LEWIS AND ST. PAUL: GOD'S SELF-GIVING LOVE

The 1993 film *Shadowlands* tells the well-known story of the Christian theologian and writer C. S. Lewis (1898–1963) marrying the American Poet Joy Davidman and their subsequent journey together through her illness and death from cancer.[8] Lewis is played by Anthony Hopkins and Davidman by Debra Winger. Directed by Richard Attenborough, the film is set at Magdalen College, Oxford, where Lewis was Professor of English literature and became famous for his children's stories *The Chronicles of Narnia* (1950–56). Other works of his such as *The Problem of Pain* (1940), *Miracles* (1947), and *Mere Christianity* (1952) ring through the film as Lewis moves from the ivory tower of his academic work to the painful experience of self-giving love and Joy's agonizing death. His experience of marriage and bereavement is expressed in *A Grief Observed* (1961). Since his death in 1963 Lewis has risen to cult status, not least in the United States. His books epitomize a certain brand of Christian faith and he is much quoted in Christian circles. There are several biographies.[9]

One of Lewis's less well-known books is *The Four Loves* (1960) which focuses on the four different kinds of love human beings experience. The book started life as radio talks during the period of Joy Davidman's illness. There are four different kinds of love, Lewis says, and they all intertwine and overlap. They all involve giving and needing which Lewis calls Gift-love and Need-love. The "four loves" themselves are as follows: first, affection. This is basically the love experienced within a family. It's the love a parent has for a child and a child for a parent. It's the love that is homely and instinctive to those around us. It's a broad, modest, ambivalent, humble type of love. It does not discriminate and can bring a variety of different people into its orbit, including people we don't actually like but who deserve our affection. It also stretches to animals of different kinds who might be part of our family. But there's more to love than affection.

Lewis's second type of love is friendship. This is a more spiritual type of love which is related to companionship. It is characterized by a common interest or pursuit. We love friends because we share something with them, see things in the same way as they do or enjoy a common activity. Two friends look at something else beyond themselves and the friendship

---

8. See the film directed by Attenborough, *Shadowlands*. Joy Davidman uses her married name Gresham in the movie.

9. C. S. Lewis's works are widely available. For a recent biography see McGrath, *C. S. Lewis*.

is rooted in this. Friendship stretches beyond family, is less needy, and is unnecessary. It can be exclusive and proud. The third type of love Lewis identifies is romantic love or *eros*. There's a difference here, he says, from common contemporary usage in which *eros* means sexual love. Lewis distinguishes romantic love from sexual love which he calls Venus. Romantic love is being "in love." It's the kind of love we fall into and which can consume us. It may include physical love and the other loves but it may not include them at all. It can be focused completely on another person whereas sexual love can be totally inward looking. And romantic love can free sexual love from self-obsession.

Lewis calls the fourth type of love "charity." This word can be misleading because of its association with giving to good causes. It's very much more than that. Charity is the most important of the four loves and although it does contain the fundamental element of giving, it's a completely selfless love. This love is the self-giving, heart-breaking love of God (cf. 1 John 4:7–8). It's a disinterested love that wants only what's best for the other. God is one who gives freely and indeed creates freely not for his own benefit but totally for the benefit of the other. This sort of love needs nothing for itself; it gives totally of itself.

In the New Testament St. Paul emphasizes the importance of love in relation to God and uses the word *agape* or "charity" (as the KJV has it) for this. Lewis doesn't include any study of 1 Corinthians 13 in his book but Paul's famous "Hymn" or "Song to Love" is basically about Lewis's fourth type; it is the sort of love God has. The first part of 1 Corinthians 13 (vv. 1–3) contrasts love with other matters such as speaking in tongues, prophecy, and knowledge. Without love, Paul says, these are empty. In vv. 4–7 something of the real essence of this type of love comes out: it is patient and kind, not arrogant or rude, not selfish, irritable or resentful. It is enduring and hopeful. In vv. 8–13 we learn that all other things that we think are important will pass away but there are three things that will not: faith, hope, and love. And then the surprising climax that love is the greatest element, even above faith. This love is like God's love: disinterested and selfless.

Shadowlands tells the story of Lewis's personal journey through an agonizing test of love during his wife's death from cancer. While she was dying, he was writing *The Four Loves* and his experience brought him into a radical confrontation with God and the meaning of his own faith. The film and the books illustrate the nature of God's own love, known in the Bible as *agape*, the selfless, self-giving, freely available love that God displays in creating us in the first place and in renewing us in Jesus Christ, whose life was also characterized by selflessness and compassion for others. This love is not self-centered or self-seeking. It's a painful, self-giving love that always seeks the well-being of the other person. It is active and outgoing, costly and valuable. This love has a price and is the basis of freedom and new life for lover and beloved alike. This love is more than affection, friendship or romantic/sexual love. It is what Lewis, St. Paul, and Christians all over the world experience as the love of God.

Bible Study Passages

Lev 19:18 / Deut 6:4–5

1 Cor 13

1 John 4:7–21

Questions for Discussion

Share anything you know about C. S. Lewis and his journey of faith.

What effect did the death of his wife have on Lewis?

Discuss the different sorts of love you know about.

What is the love of God like?

What is the relation between love and faith?

Further Reading

Lewis, C. S. *The Four Loves*. New York: HarperCollins, 2012.

Wright, Tom. *Paul for Everyone: 1 Corinthians*. London: SPCK, 2014.

FIRST AND SECOND CORINTHIANS: STRENGTH AND WEAKNESS

In his well-known TV documentary *A History of Christianity* (based on his book of the same name) the Oxford Professor of the History of the Church Diarmaid MacCulloch presents a fascinating history of the Christian faith in all its many different dimensions since the outset.[10] He covers

---

10. For the book and the DVD, see MacCulloch, *History*.

Part 2: Living Faith

the beginnings in Jerusalem, different strands within early Christianity as it spread in various directions, the split between East and West, the dramatic divisions of the period of the European Reformation, and the kaleidoscope of modern denominations. During the six episodes, viewers become aware of some of the many Orthodox Churches, the Roman Catholic Church, the Protestant and Reformed Churches, and the different groups known particularly in the United States, such as the Mennonites and the Amish. It is easy to wonder at the end of the programs what holds all the churches together. Indeed, at one point, MacCulloch suggests that it might be better to think of "Christianities" rather than "Christianity." Many modern scholars would agree that there has never been a single entity called Christianity: there have been competing strands within it from the beginning.

So, is it in fact possible to say what the Christian gospel is really all about? I believe St. Paul gives us an answer in his two letters to the Christians in Corinth, written in the middle years of the first century. In his first letter, Paul is responding to various problems that have arisen in the community, not least major divisions (1:10–17), issues relating to immorality (5:1–2), marriage and divorce (7:1–16), worship (11:2–33), and theological matters such as the resurrection (15:1–58). By way of response, Paul says that the wisdom of God is different from that of human beings, making the point that God's wisdom looks like foolishness to human beings (1:18–31; 2:1–8). This idea of the "foolishness of God" forms the backbone of Paul's theology. God has different ways of being in the world from human beings and the difference is the way God operates through weakness.

In 2 Corinthians Paul takes up this central theme with the greatest tenderness. In this letter he is at his most emotional, his most sincere, perhaps, and his most personal. He is also at his most profound. In this second letter, Paul is faced with a new round of problems, the main one of which is a group of what he calls "super-apostles" or "false apostles" (11:5, 13; 12:11) who have come in from the outside and seem to have been preaching "another Jesus" and a "different gospel" (11:1–6) from the one Paul preached. The main problem for Paul is that his authority and status have been challenged, and there also seems to have been a particular incident in which Paul and another person have fallen out (2:1–11; 7:12). We do not now need to know exactly what it was, but we do know that this context of bad relations is the one in which Paul strikes back at those with whom he has come into conflict. And he strikes back with the message of God's weakness as found in Jesus Christ.

Paul says that he himself has undergone great pain and suffering on behalf of the Corinthians (11:22–29). The "super-apostles" seem to have gone to Corinth with their "other gospel" carrying letters of recommendation (3:1). They have perhaps gone from the Jerusalem church and might have been Judaizers or gnostics. But Paul's main complaint is that they seem to be setting themselves up as authoritative on the basis of their own human credentials (10:18). To them he emphasizes his own Christ-centered gospel: it is about humility and weakness. Paul says, "For we do not proclaim ourselves; we proclaim Jesus Christ as Lord" (4:5). He prides himself on Christ and not on human strength (5:12–15). He stresses Christ's weakness and links it to his own. Christ chose to become weak even though he was rich (8:9). And Paul adds, "Whenever I am weak, then I am strong" (12:10). Paul's suffering has put him at one with Christ and his experience has told him that this is the heart of the gospel. This inversion of values turns worldly power upside down and makes weakness powerful. Those who show off, seeking human and worldly power, he says, are "false apostles" full of their own pride. The same message can be found in Philippians 2:6–11 where Paul writes of Christ being "in the form of God" but "taking the form of a slave." Paul's experience tells him that there is a real strength in weakness which is unknown to some but which characterizes the gospel. And this is certainly in line with the humility and compassion of Jesus himself as reflected in the gospels.

By the end of Professor Diarmaid MacCulloch's TV programs, the viewer has visited many exotic locations around the world and met an array of larger-than-life characters. And you might be left wondering what the future holds for Christianity as well as what the past was all about. The many competing strands within Christianity make it difficult to find a common thread. The words of T. S. Eliot come quickly to mind: "Christianity is always adapting itself into something which can be believed."[11] This might be true at the level of culture and practice but Paul's contribution surely suggests something more fundamental to Christian identity.

In 1 and 2 Corinthians Paul's theology was formed in the context of a serious controversy over truth and authority and has a real ring of authenticity about it. For him Christianity is really all about the strength and power of weakness. And that weakness is the real power because in it we are freed from all the pride and arrogance of our own selves and of the world. For Paul, the real gospel turns the world upside down and changes values.

11. Quoted in Hick, *Myth*, ix.

Weakness becomes strength and foolishness becomes wisdom. This is the real power of the gospel for Paul and the center of his theology of the death and resurrection of Christ. This is what Christianity is all about because it is what God, as seen in Jesus, is all about.

Bible Study Passages

1 Cor 1:10–17

2 Cor 8:9

2 Cor 12:1–10

Questions for Discussion

How fair is it to say that there are many different "Christianities"?

What is the common thread that holds all Christians together?

How does St. Paul react to the problem of splits in the Church in Corinth?

Is Paul right that weakness is a strength?

What are your experiences of finding wisdom in foolishness?

Further Reading

Keener, Craig. *1–2 Corinthians*. Cambridge: Cambridge University Press, 2010.

Kim, Yung Suk. *Messiah in Weakness: A Portrait of Jesus from the Perspective of the Dispossessed*. Eugene, OR: Cascade, 2016.

THE FISH: RESURRECTION JOURNEY

You must have seen it! On stickers on the backs of cars, on people's T-shirts and coats, as earrings and key rings, and in ancient mosaics and frescoes all over the world. It's the fish, the symbol indicating that someone is a Christian. It's the symbol of disciples and followers of Jesus. It's widely seen and widely known, and has been used for centuries by Christians in many different countries.

The Bible is full of fish, with some fascinating and powerful uses of the image. Fish are already important in the gospels. Some of the disciples were fishermen and life around the Sea of Galilee inevitably involved catching and eating fish (Mark 1:16–20). Jesus says he wants the disciples to "fish for people" (v. 17) and some of his miracles involve fish (6:35–44; 8:1–10). In the resurrection appearance stories, fish are especially noticeable: in John's gospel they are in abundance in the miraculous catch (21:1–14) and in Luke, Jesus eats fish following the journey along the Road to Emmaus (24:43). What is the symbolism of the fish and where did it come from?

Fish live in water and both water and fish appear in numerous places in the Bible. They are symbols of new life. Water plays an important part in the opening of the book of Genesis and is part of God's initial creative acts (1:2, 6–7). In the book of Jonah, a "large fish" plays an important part (1:17) in God's purposes for the people of Nineveh. And when it comes to the visions of the end of time, Ezekiel sees water flowing from the temple in Jerusalem down the Arava valley and into the Dead Sea. And the water has many different kinds of fish in it (Ezek 47:1–12; cf. Zech 14:8). It is clear in this literature that water and fish symbolize creation, healing, and new creation as God works out his purposes.

One less well-known story containing a fish is told in the book of Tobit in the Apocrypha. During the period of the exile, Tobit and his wife, Anna, send their son, Tobias, to Media to collect money from relatives. Someone called Azarias goes with him and only the reader knows that he is really the Angel Raffaele. On the journey they sit down on a river bank and a fish jumps up out of the water. They decide to eat it but to save its heart, liver, and gall which they take with them. When they get to Media to the house of Raguel and Edna, Tobias falls in love with their daughter Sarah, whom he wants to marry. Unfortunately, she has had seven husbands before and has a curse on her. Each husband has died on the wedding night in the bridal chamber. Tobias is told that if takes the heart and the liver of the fish into the bedroom he will live. He does this and is still alive the next morning! When he gets back home, he finds that his father, Tobit, has lost his sight, but Tobias is able to heal him with the gall of the fish. At the end of the story, the exiled family returns to Israel and it is clear that the journey with the fish has brought new life, health, and restoration.

The story of the book of Tobit has been made popular in recent times by Salley Vickers' novel *Miss Garnet's Angel*. Following a lifetime of teaching and the loss of a friend, Miss Garnet sets off to the watery city of Venice, Italy, where she wanders into the Church of St. Raffaele and sees the story of the book of Tobit illustrated in frescoes on the church's walls. The story of Tobias's journey with its healing and restoration is mirrored by Miss Garnet's own journey toward healing and a new experience and perception of life.

In the Gospel of Luke, Jesus' ministry and mission are very much part of a journey (9:51—19:28) as are the resurrection appearances in the last chapter. Following the journey along the Emmaus Road (24:13–35) Jesus gathers his disciples and eats fish (24:36–43). It is possible that the story of Tobit influenced the ending of Luke's gospel. In the case of the Tobit story, Azarias travels and eats fish, though we are told at the end that he did not really eat the fish because he's an angel. In Luke's gospel Jesus really does eat the fish, indicating that he is more than an angel (Luke 24:43; cf. Heb 1:1–14). In both places the themes of the journey and the fish are foremost, symbolizing God's process of creation and re-creation, of healing, new life, and resurrection.

Wherever you see it, the fish is the symbol of Christians: the stickers on car windscreens, the T-shirts, the key rings or the ancient frescoes and mosaics. The fish is the symbol of followers of Jesus, reminding us that we are people of new life, healing and resurrection. We are part of God's purposes in creation and re-creation as he moves everything toward its ultimate perfection. It has often been said that the Christian life is a journey and as we follow Jesus, the fish is a powerful symbol of our journeying. As we travel through all the ups and downs of life with its challenges and difficulties, the fish reminds us that we travel from exile to the promised land, from illness toward healing and wholeness, from death to life and resurrection. In the second century, the African theologian Tertullian (ca. 160–ca. 225) brought the images of fish and water together in a striking way. Christians are like fish, he says, because they're "born in water," a lovely image reminding us of our baptism into Christ and of all that this involves.[12] Considering all its associations, there's no wonder the fish came to symbolize the salvation brought through Jesus. Indeed, the initial letters of the words "Jesus Christ, Son of God, Savior" in Greek spell the word *icthus*, which means "fish."

Bible Study Passages

Ezek 47:1–12

Luke 24:36–49

John 21:1–14

---

12. See Tertullian, *On Baptism*, 6.

Questions for Discussion

Where have you seen the fish as a symbol of Christians?

Why do you think the fish is such a popular symbol?

What is the significance of water as a symbol?

In what ways do the gospels use the fish symbol?

What other symbols would you use for Christians?

Further Reading

Kelly, Anthony J. *The Resurrection Effect: Transforming Christian Life and Thought*. New York: Orbis, 2008.

Vickers, Salley. *Miss Garnet's Angel*. New York: HarperCollins, 2000.

PATMOS: THE NEW CREATION

The Greek island of Patmos lies in the Aegean Sea in the northern part of the collection of islands known as the Dodecanese. From the monastery at one of the highest points on the island the views are staggering. On a clear day, everything seems perfect with the radiant blue of the sea, the lush green of the trees, and the pure white buildings shimmering in the bright sunlight. It's not difficult to imagine a religious experience or a vision there. You can easily see creation cleansed and refreshed: the "new creation," perhaps, of Christian hope and expectation.

Patmos is the island tradition associates with the Apostle John and the New Testament book of Revelation. Indeed, the book itself states clearly that this is where John's vision took place (1:9). According to later tradition, following his vision, the apostle went to Ephesus (in present-day Turkey) and lived there until he died at a great age. The monastery of St. John the Theologian on Patmos goes back to the late eleventh century and was founded by St. Christodulus with permission from the Byzantine Emperor Alexis Comnenus (1081–1118). The focus of Christian pilgrimages to Patmos these days is the cave of the apostle in which tradition locates the vision. In the sacred enclave, the seer knelt in prayer and put his hand in the wall to steady himself as he got up. In the stunning silence and beauty to be found there still today, one can imagine John's vision of a new heaven and a new earth (21:1).

PART 2: LIVING FAITH

The book of Revelation is a most mysterious work. The Greek word for "revelation" is "apocalypse," meaning "turning back" or "uncovering," and this is one of the book's other names. Apocalyptic literature is well known for its visionary, dream-like qualities. The book of Daniel is the Old Testament parallel to Revelation and is also visionary in its basic outlook. The many layers of this type of literature are saturated with views of another world, and with vivid multilayered imagery, symbols, and dramatic events carrying multiple meanings. No wonder the book of Revelation has been so variously interpreted. Some have seen it as the most Christian book of the New Testament carrying dramatic imagery of the divinity of Christ. Others have seen it as a betrayal of everything Christ stood for. The English novelist D. H. Lawrence famously compared its place among the New Testament writings to that of Judas among Jesus' disciples.[13] Ancient and modern political interpretations have been many and varied.

But even though there are numerous layers of meaning in this book, the main thing is the vision: an insight into God's ways with the world; a vision of what is to come through Christ and what will be at the end of time. After the opening address and the account of the vision (ch. 1), the book begins with the famous Letters to the Seven Churches (2–3). Then there's another vision of heaven (4) and of the Lamb (who is Christ) opening the seals of the scroll (5). The preliminaries to the end of time then follow with horses, an earthquake, and the moon like blood (6–7). Then another seal is opened: there are angels and trumpets, thunder and lightning, the woman clothed with the sun, and the dragon and the beasts (8–14). Finally, the coming of the end itself with the sea of glass, visions of doom, the fall of Babylon, the destruction of the devil, and the visions of glory and of the Book of Life (15–20). All this is followed by the vision of the new creation in chapter 21.

The vision is of a renewed heaven and earth. It is a vision of the New Jerusalem (with all its associations from the past) coming down from heaven. We are soon told that the first heaven and earth have passed away and that "the sea was no more" (21:1). In biblical literature, the sea indicates pre-creation chaos and the fact that the writer of Revelation takes the trouble to say that there is no more sea indicates that the new creation is free from chaos and evil. The new creation is what God always intended creation to be. And now God makes "all things new" (v. 5). Again, the city is seen coming down from heaven radiating God's glory (v. 10–11). The

---

13. Lawrence, *Apocalypse*, 67.

chapter recalls Ezekiel's vision of the new temple (Ezek 40–48) but we are now told that the New Jerusalem at the end of time will have no temple because God and Christ, symbolized by the Lamb, are the new temple (v. 22). Indeed, the lamp of the new city is the Lamb (v. 23) and there will be no night there (v. 25). The entire chapter provides a climax to the book showing that John's vision is one of creation as it should be: without sea, temple or night, perfect and whole without evil or chaos.

The island of Patmos is a stunningly beautiful location for a vision of God and for an insight into what the world could be like and hopefully will be like at the end of time. It is an ideal place for a vision of the new creation. Though not without its violent history, the island breathes a sense of peace and perfection. The notion of moving toward a renewed creation is fundamental to the book of Revelation and to a great deal of eastern Christian theology. And the insight can already be found in the writings of St. Paul: "So if anyone is in Christ, there is a new creation: everything old has passed away; see, everything has become new!" (2 Cor 5:17; see also, Gal 6:15; cf. Col 3:10).

The notion of God renewing creation is still fundamental to the Christian vision of the world today and to the Christian understanding of God's ultimate purposes for it. It is a crucial vision in matters of ecological, environmental, and political concern; in matters of family and social life; in matters of education, training, and justice. We move forward inspired by a vision like that of John of Patmos, a vision that gives us hopeful insight into the way God wants the world to be.

Bible Study Passages

2 Cor 5:17–19

Col 3:1–11

Rev 21:1–4

Questions for Discussion

Discuss places where you have experienced a sense of perfection and completion.

How does the writer of Revelation use the images of the sea and the temple?

Share experiences of evil and chaos in the world.

PART 2: LIVING FAITH

In what ways does Jesus make creation "new"?

How can Christians help to "renew" creation?

Further Reading

Boxall, Ian. *Revelation: Vision and Insight; An Introduction to the Apocalypse.* London: SPCK, 2002.

Gunton, Colin E. *Christ and Creation.* Eugene, OR: Wipf and Stock, 2005.

4

Christian Life

EPHPHATHA: BE OPENED!

THE STORY IN MARK 7:31–37 in which Jesus heals a deaf man who also has an impediment in his speech is one of the most interesting and revealing in the gospels. A number of things are immediately noticeable. The healing of the Syrophoenician woman comes just before it and establishes Jesus' significance outside the land of Israel (7:24–30). We are then told that Jesus continues in the Decapolis, a Gentile area, which reinforces the same theme (v. 31). The following Feeding of the Four Thousand is also in line with this (8:1–10). Jesus is obviously a boundary-breaker with a message for Gentiles as well as Jews. He also clearly fulfils prophecy: Isaiah had spoken centuries before of the opening of mouths and ears at the end of time (see Isa 29:18; 32:3; 35:5). And indeed, Mark 7:31–37 is not the only story in this gospel which shows Jesus giving sight to the blind: there's the gradual healing of the Blind Man of Bethsaida for whom men look like trees (8:22–26) and the healing of the blind beggar Bartimaeus in Jericho (10:46–52). Other things are noticeable in Mark 7:31–37 too, especially the use of spittle in healing the man. In the ancient world, spittle was thought to have healing qualities.

But one of the most interesting elements in this story is the use of the Aramaic word *ephphatha*. Jesus puts his fingers into the man's ears and says *ephphatha*: "be opened." There are other occasions in Mark's gospel when Aramaic is used and they are all particularly dramatic moments (5:41; 15:34). On this occasion the Aramaic word has to do with the opening of the man's ears. At the simplest level, he is deaf and cannot hear the message of Jesus. But there is also a deeper level of deafness. The man symbolizes others in the gospel story who are not physically deaf but who "cannot hear." There has already been significant emphasis by Mark in the Parable of the Sower on those who need to listen and those who hear but do not understand (4:3, 9, 12). Clearly deafness is a key theme in receiving the good news of the gospel—or failing to do so.

It was Plutarch who originally pointed out that we have been given one tongue but two ears and that therefore we should do twice as much listening as talking! The saying is sometimes quoted these days although it is interesting to note how listening and silence are still greatly needed and misunderstood in our society. Musicians are perhaps the ones who are most aware of how important listening is, both to themselves and to each other, and of just how little listening goes on at the general level. The distinction between hearing and listening is very important for there is certainly a great deal "heard" these days as our society bludgeons us with data through technological media. But it is doubtful whether much actual listening goes on at the deeper level of really appreciating. It is ironical that a culture which has so many listening devices is not well trained in actually listening at a deep level. Even those who have music on all day might not actually have much in-depth acoustic ability.

Plutarch's adage has another level, brought out by the simple observation of the growth of the human body in the womb. The contrast now is between the eye and the ear. In the development of the human fetus in the womb before birth, the ear functions first after about forty-five days which is about seven and a half months before the eye.[1] This remarkable fact underlines the priority of the ear, and yet in our society it is the eye that is given precedence as the primary vehicle of knowledge. Sight is taken to be superior to hearing: it gives us knowledge, while hearing tells us nothing. But this is completely wrong. Truth comes also through the organ which develops first. People seem incapable of listening to each other, of developing good aural ability, and of appreciating the value of hearing as a medium of knowledge. This is illustrated by the increasing lack of music being taught in primary schools. There are many ways in which a real appreciation of the importance of the ear and of listening would make a difference to the way we generally perceive and understand the world.

Ephphatha: "be opened." How would the opening of our ears give us a better chance of understanding our faith and religion? Why is listening such an important part of faith? First, it is important to remember that all

---

1. See Barenboim, *Everything Is Connected*.

our senses put us in touch with creation, the world of nature, and what is going on in it. It's always a danger to absolutize one or two of the senses such as the sight or touch. If this happens, the other senses tend to get reduced to nothing. Sight is often linked with the mind and then absolutized, eliminating the significance of the other senses. There always needs to be, therefore, a balance of the senses in the way we perceive the world and understand it. Seeing, hearing, touching, tasting, and smelling all need to play a part along with our minds and emotions. And if this is true of our reading of the world of creation, it is also true of our experience of God. God comes to us through our various senses. This is part of the strength of the Orthodox and Catholic liturgies as traditionally understood: they engage all the senses at once.

This is one of the key factors in the story of the man in Mark 7:31–37. His ears are opened. And when our ears are opened, we start to hear different things. When we hear more, we get in touch not only with the many different levels of God's life but also with his coming to us in music and in conversation. When we listen—to God's silence, to each other and to music—we hear the presence of God in fuller and deeper ways. And so, it lies at the heart of the Christian gospel that we must not be deaf to God. *Ephphatha*: "be opened"!

Bible Study Passages

Isa 35:5–7

Mark 4:10–12

Mark 7:31–37

Questions for Discussion

Discuss the importance of listening and hearing.

Why has seeing become more important than hearing?

How can the use of all our senses tell us more about the world and about God?

What are your impressions of the account of Jesus opening the man's ears?

How can more attention to hearing help us understand and communicate our faith today?

PART 2: LIVING FAITH

Further Reading

Begbie, Jeremy. *Music, Modernity, and God: Essays in Listening*. Oxford: Oxford University Press, 2013.

Hooker, Morna D. *The Gospel according to Saint Mark*. Grand Rapids: Baker, 2011.

PADDINGTON BEAR: A NEW FAMILY

In a busy corner of Paddington station in London, amid the hustle and bustle of shops, cafés, travelers, and trains there stands the famous statue of Paddington Bear. Sculpted by Marcus Cornish in bronze, it appeared in the station in the year 2000. The bear is, of course, the one made famous by Michael Bond in his twenty or so children's books published from 1958 onward and known to thousands of children and adults ever since. The appearance of a film about Paddington in 2014, and now a sequel, have made him even more famous.[2] The cult of this wonderful and adventurous creature continues to spread and there is now a shop at Paddington Station selling all manner of Paddington merchandise.

The basic story is well known from Bond's first book, *A Bear Called Paddington*.[3] One day Mr. and Mrs. Brown go to Paddington Station to meet their daughter Judy, who is coming home from school. Mr. Brown thinks he sees a bear in the corner of the station and Mrs. Brown thinks he's losing his head. When they get nearer, they discover that there is indeed a bear sitting on the ground with a suitcase and a tag on him saying, "Please look after this bear." It turns out that the bear has come all the way from darkest Peru and has left his Aunt Lucy behind in a retirement home for bears. The Browns feel very sorry for the bear and take him home with them. Because of the location where they found him, they decide to call him Paddington. And so, Paddington goes home with them, thus beginning many an exciting and challenging escapade in the Brown household. One thing is for sure: the Brown family will never be the same again.

Families are important. But who do we think of as our family? We probably think, first of all, of our immediate families: mothers, fathers, sisters, and brothers. Then there's the wider family: aunts and uncles, cousins,

---

2. The books by Michael Bond are widely available. See also the films directed by King, *Paddington*.

3. Bond, *Paddington*.

and others we perhaps don't see that often. Then there's our more distant family, perhaps through marriage. And then there are people we know are there but have probably never met and never think of as family. Maybe they're distant cousins once or twice removed. And in what ways do we belong to the family of England or Europe or the human family? And at the other extreme, are there friends that we think of as family because they're so close? Sometimes friends are closer than family. Families are important in all human societies and cultures and they have played a key part right down through the millennia of human existence. They have been part of human experience from the beginning and have formed part of the structure of human communities all over the world for generations.

In the period of the Old Testament there are several layers to family groups. First of all, people belonged to their "family," which usually had the sense of the extended family. Then there was the "clan," which consisted of a number of extended families. Then there was the "tribe," which consisted of a number of clans. We are familiar with the twelve tribes of Israel, for example Dan, Benjamin, Manasseh, and Asher. The twelve tribes gave the Israelites a sort of outer layer of identity (Josh 13:1—21:45). Your tribe, clan, and family gave you identity in geographical and economic terms. The family unit is also evident in the New Testament. For example, in Acts when people are converted, it's often the whole family that's involved. When Cornelius is converted in Acts 10:1–33, his whole household goes with him. When Lydia is baptized in Acts 16:11–15, her whole family is baptized as well.

However, already in the letters of Paul we hear that for Christians things are different. Family is one of the areas in which the message and impact of Jesus changes something quite radically. In Ephesians 2:19 the author speaks of the "household of God" indicating that there is now another way of thinking about family. Also, in Galatians 6:10 Paul writes, "So then, whenever we have an opportunity, let us work for the good of all, and especially for those of the family of faith" (cf. 1 Tim 3:15; 1 Pet 4:17). Now, there is a new family or unit of identity defined by faith in Jesus. In Hebrews 3:1–6 the image of the house is used to show how the house built by Jesus has surpassed the one built by Moses.

In the gospels there's also a strong sense of a new type of family brought about by Jesus and his message: "For I have come to set a man against his father, and a daughter against her mother, and a daughter-in-law against her mother-in-law. . . . Whoever loves father or mother more than me is not worthy of me; and whoever loves son or daughter more than me is not worthy of me" (Matt 10:35–37). This indicates that in the life of following Jesus there will be division between those who prioritize him and those who do not. But even more fundamental is the message that in following Jesus the very sense of who our family is will be changed. When we follow Jesus our family unit changes, our family identity changes, even our clan or tribe changes. Now there's a new identity and a new family. This is perhaps best summed up in Mark 3:31–35 when, confronted with his mother and brother and sisters, Jesus asks, "Who are my mother and my brothers? . . . Here are my mother and my brothers! Whoever does the will of God is my brother and sister and mother."

The story of Paddington Bear shows how on that amazing day at Paddington Station the Browns were happy not only to welcome a stranger into their midst but also to reimagine their family. They take Paddington (another species!) back with them and welcome him into their home. The same challenge comes to all of us who follow Jesus. In him we belong to a new family group and inherit a new identity that sets new relationships in place and makes new demands upon us. Being in Jesus' family changes who is in our family.

Bible Study Passages

Matt 10:34–39

Mark 3:31–35

Luke 14:25–33

Questions for Discussion

Who do you normally think of as your family?

Who is definitely not in your family?

How do you feel about the idea of the "human family"?

In what ways does Jesus redefine our family?

What does the Christian family look like to you?

Further Reading

Bond, Michael. *A Bear Called Paddington*. New York: HarperCollins, 2014.

Williams, Rowan. *Meeting God in Paul*. London: SPCK, 2015.

BRIDGES OVER TROUBLED WATERS: RECONCILIATION

Many of us who grew up in the 1970s are more than familiar with the songs of Simon and Garfunkel.[4] They define a musical and cultural era and still ring through the minds and hearts of those who grew up listening to them. "Homeward Bound," "Sounds of Silence," "Mrs. Robinson," "I Am a Rock." And then, of course, the very well-known "Bridge over Troubled Water," perhaps the most defining song of them all, the one we think of as quintessentially "Simon and Garfunkel." It came out in 1970 as a single from the album of the same name and was in the charts for three weeks. Written by Paul Simon and sung by Art Garfunkel, it has remained a haunting and inspiring piece ever since. We can probably sing most of the words, and the distinctive piano accompaniment rambles through our heads for days on end after hearing it.

But did we ever actually listen to the words? Probably few of us really paid much attention to what any of the songs were about! In any case, we probably didn't think of "Bridge over Troubled Water" as a particularly religious song. But if you listen to the words carefully, it's possible to recognize that the bridge and water imagery have powerful resonances with Christianity, especially with baptism and the ministry all Christians are called to. For Christians, baptism is the entrance into a new way of life, into a calling to reconcile and heal, mend the broken and bring together the separated. Through the water of baptism, we are called to build bridges over troubled waters.

The water imagery reminds us of a number of important events in the Bible. In the gospels, Jesus' ministry begins with his baptism, though it is played down somewhat in John (Matt 3:13–17; Mark 1:9–11; Luke 3:21–22; John 1:29–34). The accounts in the first three gospels focus on the voice indicating God's presence and the dove symbolizing the Spirit. The event takes place at the River Jordan which brings to mind the events of the

---

4. Collections of their songs are widely available.

exodus, particularly the crossing of the Red Sea (Exod 14:1–31), and the crossing of the River Jordan into the new land (Josh 3:1–17).

The accounts of Jesus' baptism in the gospels thus indicate the coming of God and the Spirit in a new age and a new people, resonating with the events of Israel's past. In those places, water symbolizes freedom, liberation, and new life. And when Jesus' ministry begins, he teaches, preaches, and heals, mends and brings together, reconciles and makes new (Luke 4:14–20). In the Old Testament more generally, water, especially the sea, also symbolizes a pre-creation chaos (Ps 89:9). When Jesus stills the storm in the gospels (Mark 4:35–41), he calms the troubled water and so brings order out of chaos. His work is that of calming chaos and bringing new life. The gospels don't use the image exactly but Jesus is a bridge builder and reconciler, and the disciples are encouraged to follow in his steps (Mark 8:34).

This fundamental element in Jesus' ministry is summed up succinctly in St. Paul's words in 2 Corinthians 5:19, "in Christ God was reconciling the world to himself." Certainly, Paul's life was an example of reconciling work. In all his letters we see a life given to the service of others, a life given to bringing people together, to mending breakages in communities, and to building bridges wherever they were needed. His own life of reconciliation reflects that of God himself. Reconciliation is what God himself wants in creation as he brings it to renewal. And it is God's work that both Jesus and Paul were doing. They were both God's bridge builders. It is then a short step to see that we too as baptized Christians are called into the same ministry of reconciling and bridge building (2 Cor 5:17–21). It is our responsibility to enter into the practical working out of our faith and baptism by building bridges and calming waters in God's work of reconciliation.

The words of Simon and Garfunkel's "Bridge over Troubled Water" resonate with this Christian baptismal ministry when they speak of drying the eyes of the weary and the friendless, of helping the down-and-out and those on the street, and of being there for those who need a friend to comfort them in times of darkness. And it is most significant, perhaps, that the song speaks of the friend not just building bridges but actually being the bridge. The narrator in the song commits to laying himself down as the bridge. And so, we too are called like Jesus not just to want bridges or even to be the enablers of bridges but to be the bridges ourselves.

In the light of all this, it's perhaps not surprising to learn that "Bridge over Troubled Water" is the name of an institution (founded in 1970) that helps homeless youth in Boston, Massachusetts. The words of the song are originally an affirmation of helping the homeless and needy on the streets of Boston and they resonate powerfully with the reconciling ministry of Jesus and of all baptized Christians.

What was it that was so distinctive about Simon and Garfunkel? Their wonderfully fresh voices, their close harmonies and acoustic guitar accompaniments? Or perhaps the words of the songs themselves? Since the 1970s "Bridge over Troubled Water" has continued to be a popular song. There have been numerous covers, for example the ones by Roberta Flack, Tom Jones, Aretha Franklin, Elvis Presley, Roy Orbison, Charlotte Church, and Russell Watson among many others. The music is powerful and evocative but it's the words that are most important. They speak of reconciliation and the Christian ministry of building bridges and calming waters, bringing people out of separation and alienation back into God's life of peace with others. Long may this song be sung and long may its words be heard, for we too must be bridges over troubled waters wherever we find ourselves.

Bible Study Passages

Josh 3:1–17

Mark 4:35–41

2 Cor 5:17–21

Questions for Discussion

Discuss the words of the song "Bridge over Troubled Water."

What does the idea of building bridges mean to you?

In what ways did Jesus build bridges between people?

What are the particular responsibilities of a baptized Christian?

In what ways can Christians build bridges in your area?

Further Reading

Horsfall, Tony. *Servant Ministry: A Portrait of Christ and a Pattern for His Followers*. Oxford: BRF, 2013.

Wells, Samuel. *Nazareth Manifesto*. Hoboken, NJ: Wiley-Blackwell, 2015.

Part 2: Living Faith

MOTHER TERESA: SMALL THINGS WITH GREAT LOVE

In 1979, Mother Teresa of Calcutta was awarded the Nobel Peace Prize for her work among the poor and outcast in India and around the world. She had become well known and respected during the 1970s for her work with the poor and continued to be so throughout the '80s and '90s. Although she had her critics, she received many awards and honors from different countries and in 2016 was canonized in the Roman Catholic Church. Saint Teresa of Calcutta, as she now is, was a wonderful example of faith and good works brought together.

Mother Teresa was born in Skopje, Albania, in 1910. As a girl, she was always interested in missionary work and helping people. She soon knew she wanted to join a religious order and to help others. She joined the order of nuns known as Our Lady of Loreto, went to Ireland to train and then to India where she taught in one of the order's schools, eventually becoming head teacher. The poverty around her struck a deep note in her soul and she found herself drawn more and more to helping people in need. She founded a new community known as the Missionaries of Charity who were committed to helping the "poorest of the poor" in the streets of India. She opened institutions for the poor, the sick, the outcast, and the dying. Gradually her work and her fame spread and the order she founded took the work abroad. She herself traveled widely in search of helping the poor and her work was eventually established in over a hundred countries. In the words of Malcom Muggeridge's film and book about her, she wanted to do *Something Beautiful for God*.[5]

Mother Teresa's work was rooted in her faith. She was a Roman Catholic nun and her sense of Christ's concern for the poor was her driving vision. She saw Christ revealed in the suffering of people and saw the opportunity to help them as he had helped them. She is a fine example to us all in that the care of others and helping the poor lies at the heart of the gospel message. It is clear enough from the gospels that Jesus himself helped people. In his teaching, preaching, and healing he helped restore life in people (e.g., Mark 1:21–34). In his teaching there is a clear emphasis on helping those in need (e.g., Matt 5:38–48; 10:42; Luke 10:25–37). His own care for the poor is rooted in his own faith: the command to love both God and neighbor lies at the heart of ancient Judaism (Lev 19:18; Deut 6:4). And it is clear that the two are inherently related: loving God does not simply lead to loving

---

5. Muggeridge, *Something Beautiful*.

the neighbor, it involves it. The concern for the poor and less well-off is also there in the prophets of ancient Israel who are concerned about social justice and the plight of the poor (e.g., Isa 10:1–4; Amos 5:10–15). Jesus of Nazareth stood in a long tradition of Jewish concern to help others in the name of God.

The New Testament writers certainly bring out this emphasis in their presentation of Jesus and it can be seen in a number of different contexts. Caring for others and doing good works was always central. One good example is the question about "faith and works" in the writings of St. Paul. Paul is famous for making the apparent distinction between faith and works: "A person is justified by faith apart from works prescribed by the law," he says (Rom 3:28). In the Reformation period this was interpreted as a contrast between a private intellectual faith, on the one hand, and doing practical good works, on the other. They claimed that Paul was saying that faith is really what matters even before we do anything. If we have "faith" God will save us. Many people believe this today, partly in fear of conceding that if we emphasize "works" we might be attempting to save ourselves.

But it is doubtful that this is what St. Paul actually meant. He would not have had that modern polarity between intellect and action. He would have thought that the response to God in faith would include good works, even if not necessarily "works of the law." And there is another strand in the New Testament that seems to be saying something important and is often thought to conflict with Paul. The Letter of James is one of the most "ethical" letters in the New Testament, concerned with human behavior and lifestyle. James says that it is works that really matter and that faith on its own is dead. "You see that a person is justified by works," he says, "and not by faith alone" (Jas 2:24). Here the emphasis is firmly on what we do as Christians, not on what we believe. Probably there is more connection between Paul and James than is sometimes thought: the emphasis on good works is there in both and has been part of the Christian tradition all along. The same emphasis can be found in the letters of John where God himself is love (1 John 4:7–8, 16) and love of neighbor is again fundamental (4:19–20).

Mother Teresa of Calcutta has become a religious icon to those who admire her, and her life certainly seems to epitomize something of the way Christians should try to be. Her sense of God and his purposes was visionary. Of course, we can't all achieve what she achieved or do the great work that she did but we can take something from her example. We can help anyone in front of us who needs help. We can do any number of small acts that make a difference. This is where changes begin and where small efforts can grow into something bigger. Mother Teresa herself said, "Don't look for big things, just do small things with great love."[6] It is through this that we can make a difference to the world and through this that we become true followers of Jesus of Nazareth.

Bible Study Passages

Matt 10:40–42

Rom 3:27–31

Jas 2:14–26

Questions for Discussion

Share your impressions of Mother Teresa and her work.

What criticisms of Mother Teresa do you have?

Discuss Jesus' concern for the poor.

What does St. Paul say about "faith and works"?

Does the Letter of James contradict St. Paul?

Further Reading

Muggeridge, Malcolm. *Something Beautiful for God: Mother Teresa of Calcutta*. Oxford: Lion, 2009.

Spink, Katheryn. *Mother Teresa: An Authorised Biography*. New York: HarperCollins, 2011.

JESUS WEPT: CRYING AND SALVATION

In 1962, the American pop singer and songwriter Franki Valli and his group The Four Seasons released a song called "Big Girls Don't Cry." It was sung in a strikingly high falsetto voice for which Valli was well known. The song went to number one in the United States and in the UK for several weeks. It has had a number of covers since, and has become popular again through the recent jukebox musical *Jersey Boys: The Story of Franki Valli*

---

6. See Kolodiejchuk, *Mother Teresa*, 34.

and the Four Seasons and the film made out of it.[7] The words somehow play into the popular idea that crying is a weakness to be avoided. If big girls don't cry, then big boys certainly don't. It's something not to be admitted, not done in public. If you want to cry, take it away into a private place and don't let anyone see or hear you. Crying should not be done in company. This popular view is actually true in many cultures around the world: crying is a weakness.

It's all the more striking, then, that we're told twice in the gospels that Jesus cries: once over Jerusalem in Luke 19:41 because of the people's lack of understanding of peace; and again, at the death of his friend Lazarus in John 11:35. But in spite of the general idea that crying is a weakness, Jesus is in good company when he cries. In the Old Testament a number of great men can be found crying at crucial moments in their lives: Abraham cries at the death of his wife, Sarah (Gen 23:2); Joseph cries when he meets his brother Benjamin (Gen 43:30–31); King David cries at the news of the death of his son Absalom (2 Sam 18:33); and the prophet Jeremiah cries over the fall of Jerusalem (Lam 2:11). In the Jewish tradition, it seems, it's not that unusual for people to cry. In fact, it's a very human thing to do.

Jesus crying over the death of his friend Lazarus in John 11:35 is particularly striking and a very important lesson can be learned from this the shortest verse in the Bible: "Jesus wept."[8] The story is set in Bethany near Jerusalem. We know that Jesus used to stay there with his friends Martha, Mary, and their brother Lazarus. Jesus learns of Lazarus' death and goes to the tomb. Mary and the Jews are already weeping. The scene is one of immense grief and sorrow. It's striking that in John's gospel more than in the others, Jesus' humanity is stressed. In John chapter 4 he has been tired, thirsty, and hungry (v. 6, 7, 8). Now in chapter 11 his emotions are on display. He is "greatly disturbed in spirit and deeply moved" (v. 33, 38). We know other places too where he is moved in this way. In the next chapter his "soul is troubled" (12:27). In 11:33 and 38 the words used express deep emotion and compassion. In Greek, the words used of Mary and the Jews crying indicate loud wailing of a ritual sort. But a different word is used for Jesus' crying, indicating a deep compassionate grief.

And there's another interesting element about Jesus crying at the death of Lazarus: the position of the story in John's gospel as a whole. The Raising of Lazarus in chapter 11 forms a bookend with the narrative of

---

7. See the film directed by Eastwood, *Jersey Boys*.
8. This is the KJV and the RSV. The NRSV has "Jesus began to weep."

Jesus' own resurrection in chapter 20. The two stories of new life encase the story of Jesus' suffering, death, and resurrection to new life. Although the Last Supper scene in chapter 13 is often thought of as the beginning of the Passion Narrative, it is the Raising of Lazarus that actually triggers Jesus' arrest (11:53). In both literary and theological terms, the raising of Lazarus points to the passion of Jesus. Jesus' tears are the beginning of his journey along the way of the cross. John's stress on Jesus' humanity, his deep emotions and his tears, encased as they are in this story about new life which points forward to Jesus' own resurrection, is part of his understanding of the process of giving new life through suffering. The tears and grief are the beginning of the healing process of death and resurrection.

Crying is usually seen as a weakness, but what if it were seen as a strength? Jesus' tears should turn our embarrassment about crying on its head: if he can cry, so can we. Most of us cry when we're sad, frightened or in trouble. Most probably, like Jesus, we cry when a loved one or friend has died. Even so, we might still be ashamed to show our tears. We might cry in compassion for others in their grief, crying with them and sharing in their pain. And we might cry in joy, for there's a thin line sometimes between tears of pain and tears of joy. On all these occasions, our tears would feel different if they were thought of as a strength rather than a weakness, as a part of healing rather than of sickness.

We're all born crying. Only Zoroaster was born laughing. There's an important message for us in Jesus' tears in John 11. He not only makes crying OK but when we see his tears in their full significance as part of his passion, we also come to see their part in the process of healing and resurrection. It is said by some these days that crying is a good thing and many psychiatrists and psychologists would probably agree that it is a healing activity at the physical and emotional levels. It is also a healing process at the spiritual level. Crying brings its own healing to the soul and to the spirit. It is part of God's healing, moving us on through pain and weakness through passion and compassion to the joy of resurrection and new life. In the New Jerusalem, of course, there will be no more tears (Rev 21:4). But in the meantime, Franki Valli was surely wrong: crying is part of God's healing art, and it's OK.

Christian Life

Bible Study Passages

2 Sam 18:31–33
Luke 19:41–44
John 11:28–37

Questions for Discussion

Why is crying often thought to be a weakness?

Discuss occasions when crying has been embarrassing to you.

In what ways can crying be a strength?

Discuss the times when Jesus cries in the gospels.

What does it mean to say that crying plays a part in salvation?

Further Reading

Lutz, Tom. *Crying: The Natural and Cultural History of Tears*. New York: Norton, 1999.

Wright, Tom. *John for Everyone*. Part 2. Chs. 11–21. London: SPCK, 2002.

JESUS' PRAYER BOOK: PRAYING WITH THE PSALMS

Christians don't very often think about the Old Testament book of Psalms but this very rich Hebrew poetry can be a real resource for worship and private prayer. Of course, you'll already find psalms in regular use in Christian worship: they're used in the Eucharist and in the Offices of Morning and Evening Prayer. But they also somehow get overlooked. When they're sung in church, however beautiful the music, few people actually hear the words and even if they do there's little real appreciation of their meaning. Even when the psalms are said, the translation can obscure the meaning and the real message gets lost. And yet the psalms are among the most beautiful literature in the world. They are originally "songs" or prayers for use in the worship of ancient Israel. The Psalter was the prayer book of the second temple in Jerusalem, the temple that Jesus knew. The book of Psalms was effectively Jesus' "prayer book." And if Jesus used the psalms for prayer, we can also get to know them better and pray with them.

PART 2: LIVING FAITH

First of all, what are the psalms and where do they come from? The psalms are Jewish poetry from the period of the monarchy in ancient Israel. Traditionally they were thought to have been written by David, king of Israel, in about 1000 BCE, who sang them and accompanied them on the lyre. The Hebrew word for the psalms is *tehillim*, which means "songs," and this translates into Greek as "psalms." Most modern scholars think the psalms were not written by David but come from a later time when Israel returned to its land after the period of exile in Babylon (sixth century BCE). By the time the Jerusalem temple was rebuilt by Herod the Great (37–4 BCE) the psalms were the "prayer book" for use in worship. Later when the Torah, the Prophets, and the Writings were gathered together into the Jewish Bible, the psalms formed the first in the collection of Writings.

There are one hundred and fifty psalms in the Psalter, divided into the following five sections, possibly reflecting the fivefold division of the Torah: (1) Psalms 1–41; (2) Psalms 42–72; (3) Psalms 73–89; (4) Psalms 90–106; and (5) Psalms 107–150. These Hebrew psalms were translated into Greek in Alexandria in the second century BCE and were then numbered differently so that different English versions sometimes show different numbers. There are still a hundred and fifty overall. There might have been previous collections before the one we know as some of the psalms have specific notes attached to them such as "of David" (see 3–41), "of Korah" (see 42–49), and "of Asaph" (see 73–83). But in any case, the psalms reflect Jewish life and worship, public, and private and are clearly geared to the worship needs of people whose faith was strong but challenged by the realities of life. Hundreds of years later, it is still possible for us to grow in faith through use of the psalms.

The Old Testament scholar Walter Brueggemann has written a very attractive and useful little book on the psalms called *Spirituality of the Psalms*. It characterizes the psalms into three main theological types: (1) Psalms of Orientation; (2) Psalms of Disorientation; and (3) Psalms of New Orientation. Basically, it works like this: Psalms of Orientation are those psalms that reflect a basically stable outlook on life. They reflect an outlook that sees order in the familiar flow of events. People in this frame of mind experience a well-being in which life is comfortable, probably well-off, and happy. They probably like the world the way it is, or seems to be to them. Some psalms in this category are 1, 8, 14, 15, 19, 24, 33, 37, 104, 119, 131, 133, and 145.

Christian Life

Psalms of Disorientation change this attitude. These psalms reflect the mood of complaint and unhappiness. They arise from experiences of darkness, failure, and lack of faith. They are the opposite of stability and strength; they come from times of weakness, distress, and anger. This might be individual or corporate disorientation. These moods are present in psalms such as 13, 35, 74, 79, 86, and 137. Finally, there are Psalms of New Orientation. These are psalms that indicate a new turning, a new experience, a new burst of life out of the old. Something has turned darkness into light and mourning into joy. Brueggemann is clear that this is one of the key elements in the theology of the book of Psalms: the psalms testify to the experience that new life and growth can burst out of grief and pain. Psalms which show this turning are 30, 34, 40, 138 (personal thanksgiving), 65, 66, 124, 129 (community thanks), 29, 47, 93, 97, 98, 99, 114 (kingly rule), and 100, 103, 113, 117, 135, 146, 147, 148, 149, and 150 (Praise). Through all these experiences and moods, Brueggemann is clear that the prayer of the psalms is rooted in the concern for others and for the problems of the wider world.

In order to pray privately with the psalms, it's a good idea to sit down quietly. Take the time to settle down and enter into God's presence. Listen awhile and be still. Then take a psalm that you already know or want to know. Read it through and let it wash over you. Think about its mood and the experience it comes from. Identify key words that strike you. You might wish to take a psalm that speaks of God's care for you: "The Lord is my shepherd, I shall not want" (Ps 23:1); or one that speaks of your anger and despair: "My God, my God, why have you forsaken me?" (Ps 22:1); or one that speaks of the glory of God's presence: "How lovely is your dwelling place, O Lord of hosts!" (Ps 84:1). Through using the psalms in this way and letting them breathe through us, we can enter their world and let them transform us as we live out our faith in a difficult and often depressing context. After centuries of use, and sometimes of neglect, the psalms can still be a tremendous resource for our faith and worship today.

Bible Study Passages

Ps 8

Ps 13

Ps 30

PART 2: LIVING FAITH

Questions for Discussion

Where did you first hear or read the psalms?

Which are your favorite psalms and why?

Discuss the fact that the book of Psalms is Jewish.

In what ways can the psalms be used in Christian prayer?

Select a psalm and identify its key themes and emphases.

Further Reading

Brueggemann, Walter. *Spirituality of the Psalms*. Minneapolis: Fortress, 2002.

Wansbrough, Henry. *The Psalms: A Commentary for Prayer and Reflection*. Oxford: BRF, 2014.

BE'ER SHEVA: DOING JUSTICE

If you visit the archaeological site at Be'er Sheva (biblical Beer-sheba) in the Negev desert in southern Israel, you'll soon get a superb understanding of an ancient city and its workings. The Tel (or mound) is small enough for it to make sense to anyone without archaeological training. Beer-sheba is the famous southern border of ancient Israel parallel to Dan in the North: "from Dan to Beer-sheba" (e.g., Judg 20:1; 1 Sam 3:20), and is famous for being the location of Abraham's covenant with Abimelech (Gen 21:25–34). The site was excavated by the Tel Aviv Institute of Archaeology in the 1960s and '70s under the direction of Yohanan Aharoni and Ze'ev Herzog. In 2005 Tel Be'er Sheva was declared a World Heritage site by UNESCO. From the Tel there are superb views of the surrounding region. But there are deeper messages here as well: about the justice of God.

In the biblical period, Beer-sheba was a small administrative town (2.8 acres) used for governing the southern border of Israel. Ordinary people lived in houses farther afield. Most of what remains today comes from the eighth century BCE and from the top of the observation tower you can see a number of things very clearly: remains of a governor's residence, storehouses, streets, houses, and a casemate wall surrounding the whole city. There's a famous water system too and a copy of a horned altar found at the site. One of the most striking things, however, is the city gateway.

CHRISTIAN LIFE

It's a double gate in which there were obviously rooms with benches for people to sit on. This type of gate is a familiar feature of ancient Israelite cities. As you enter the site, you pass through this gate and it is worth pausing for a moment.

As the main or only point of access to the city, the gate was the place where the city was guarded. It was the point of security and defense, and indeed of vulnerability. It was the place where enemies attacked. It was the place where business transactions were carried out and legal battles fought. It was the place where prophets and occasionally kings appeared to make public announcements. It was the place where criminals were caught going in and out. It was the place from which the entire population and activity of the city could be controlled. And it was the place, therefore, where justice was established. The gate had both literal and metaphorical significance: the law court was actually set up in the gateway and people were questioned and tried there. And for this reason, the gate was also symbolic of justice. The prophet Amos says, "Hate evil and love good, and establish justice in the gate" (5:15), meaning in the city, in the community, and in society.

What is "justice" and what are we to understand by the word? In English today it has a broad variety of meanings: we often want to "see justice done" or to "do justice" to something. We think that there should be justice in personal relations and in society and associate this with law courts and government. But the average person might find it hard to give a definition of what justice is. Too often we use the word to mean "getting our own back" and assume that justice has been done when the "punishment fits the crime" in some legal battle.

In the Hebrew Bible the word "justice" has an even broader set of associations. It certainly has to do with governing, ruling, and judging: implementing the laws, practices, and customs of the country including punishing, vindicating, and delivering. More often than not, justice is connected to social relations especially in terms of "rights." This comes out especially in the concern the prophets have for the poor. Most well known are the criticisms made by Isaiah (1:16-17; 3:15; 10:1-4), Amos (5:10-24), and Micah (3:9-12) when they attack rich people who have no concern for the poor. Amos is concerned to see "justice roll down like waters, and righteousness like an ever-flowing stream" (5:24). The prophet Micah underlines this when he says, "What does the Lord require of you but to do justice, and to love kindness, and to walk humbly with your God?" (6:8).

The story of Naboth and his vineyard in 1 Kings 21 presents a particularly sharp case of social injustice to which the prophet Elijah responds.

But the word "justice" is also used with wider meanings: it can refer to harmony and wholeness in creation. It is connected to God and his character, and in this respect is part of God's basic purposes for his people (Deut 32:4; Isa 5:16). As creator and judge, God wills harmony which is connected to peace (*shalom*) for the whole earth. The practice of the Jubilee (leaving land fallow and writing off debts) every fifty years illustrates something of this connection (Lev 25). Thus, the first sense of the word should certainly be seen in the context of the second: God's justice involves human rights because they are part of God's desire for justice in the whole of creation. The teaching of Jesus in the Sermon on the Mount (Matt 5–7) contributes another angle to the complex question of the nature of God's justice.

A visit to Tel Be'er Sheva in southern Israel is an exciting archaeological experience and a great deal can be learned from it about the history of ancient Israel. But to pause in the gate and consider prophetic and other texts takes you straight to the heart of the theology of ancient Israel. And this is still the message of the Beer-sheba gate for today. It is clear that establishing justice involves making sure that legal matters are settled, and protecting human rights in society. But all this must be seen in terms of God's wider concern for the justice of the earth, the environment, and the whole of creation. God wishes to see harmony and wholeness in everything, and because of his nature and character it is the responsibility of those in society to ensure that God's justice is done, in the broader sense, throughout the earth. Indeed, this is all part of his covenant with creation and humanity, and is as important for Christians today as it was for the ancient Israelites. Establishing God's justice "in the gate" and in the whole earth remains a key responsibility for us all.

Bible Study Passages

Gen 21:25–34

1 Kgs 21:1–27

Matt 5:1–12

Questions for Discussion

What does the word "justice" mean to you?

Give examples of things that are "unjust."

What is the relation between covenant and justice?

What does it mean to say that justice is part of God's character?

How can Christians help to see justice done today?

Further Reading

Hebden, Keith. *Seeking Justice: The Radical Compassion of Jesus*. Christian Alternative, 2013.

Keller, Timothy. *Generous Justice: How God's Grace Makes Us Just*. London: Hodder, 2010.

THE LAST THINGS: WORK IN PROGRESS

Visitors to Salisbury in Wiltshire, England, usually head straight for the cathedral to see its famous spire, stunning interior, and various works of art. But if you head for the Church of St. Thomas à Becket in the center of town, you'll see the building that was erected for use by the masons who built the cathedral in the twelfth century. Inside this church is England's largest Doom painting depicting the scene of the last judgment based on the book of Revelation. Christ sits on a rainbow, arms outstretched, with the twelve apostles under him, judging the twelve tribes of Israel and deciding who will go to heaven and who to hell. Mary sits on the right and St. John on the left. The city of Jerusalem lies behind. The dead are coming up out of their graves assisted by angels with trumpets. On the left are those who are going up to heaven. On the right those who are on their way down to hell, symbolized by a huge dragon with its mouth open. Among the damned is a bishop wearing a miter! At the bottom of the right-hand side, not far away, is the vicar's stall!

The Salisbury Doom, like hundreds of others, was whitewashed at the Reformation. It was discovered in 1819 and cleaned off, and then whitewashed again and only finally rediscovered and restored in the later nineteenth century. It is a treasure of its sort in both scope and size. The so-called "Last Things" are: death, judgment, heaven, and hell. But does

God really will that there should be such a final division with some going down to eternal torment? Or are his intentions for us not more benign, optimistic, and hopeful? In the Christian tradition, some theologians have maintained that God's purpose is to save everyone from the fires of hell and destruction. Two things are important here: one is that the Christian understanding about heaven and hell isn't just about the future. It's as much about the present. And second, in the present moment we human beings can create our own heaven and hell here on earth. In fact, the Salisbury Doom is just as much about our responsibilities now as about what God has in store for us in the future.

Notions of heaven and hell certainly permeate the Bible although God and the devil are closer to each other than is often thought. In the book of Job, the devil appears in cahoots with God (1:6–12). In Psalm 139:8 God is thought of as being in heaven and in hell. The idea of hell had physical associations too: to this day a valley in Jerusalem is known as hell, Gehenna, Hades or Sheol. In the time of Solomon, it was associated with the horror of child sacrifice. Heaven certainly features in the story of Jacob's ladder in which a link is opened up between earth and heaven (Gen 28:10–22). And on Sinai, God descends from another realm in smoke and fire to visit his people (Exod 19:18; 20:22).

In the New Testament, ideas of heaven and hell are clearer. In passages which deal with the "after life" and the "end of time," notions of life with God and of torment without him are evident. The parable of the Rich Man and Lazarus shows a clear division between the rich man who goes to torment and the poor man who goes to heaven (Luke 16:19–31). In Matthew's gospel there are frequent references to the place of "weeping and gnashing of teeth" and to the different places to which people might eventually go (e.g., 8:12; 18:9). The best example is in the great chapter of judgment at the end of time in Matthew 25:31–46. And yet the wider context shows that these writers are concerned not just with judgment at the end of time but with life as it should be lived in the present. Matthew certainly knows this (chs. 5–7) and the author of Ephesians reminds Christians of their constant fight with evil and darkness (Eph 6:10–20).

Alongside the black and white, polarizing ("heaven and hell") view of God, then, the Christian tradition also has a more benign view: creation is basically good (Gen 1:10, 25, 31); it is a process in which God is working out his long-term purpose; and because God is good and wills the best for everything he has created, he moves creation in the direction of goodness at all times. Far from being a terrifying judge at the end of time, God is always sifting those he loves and preparing them for life with him. On this view, hell is more of a temporary state in which people await further processing until they are all finally "saved." Writers such as Clement (ca. 150–ca. 215), Origen (ca. 185–ca. 254), and the Cappadocian Gregory of Nyssa (ca. 330–ca. 395) held this view. And it was also maintained by some of the Reformed groups which emerged in the sixteenth century, such as the Anabaptists, the Presbyterians, and the Christadelphians. More recently F. D. E. Schleiermacher (1768–1834) in Germany and F. D. Maurice (1805–1872) in England maintained this notion of "universalism": that in the end God will save everyone from the fires of hell. The point, of course, is not that God will simply and automatically eventually "save" everyone regardless, but that he wants everyone to grow into his likeness.

The "Salisbury Doom" is certainly worth a visit.[9] Its message is more challenging than might at first seem the case. Not just about something in the distant future, it asks us to look at how we live now. It raises fundamental questions not only about how we think of the end of time and of life after death, but also about how we imagine God and his purposes in creation in the present. The painting is not just about final "doom and gloom" for those who deserve it but about God's continuing process of sifting and refining us until he works out his final purposes for us. The painting represents a demanding challenge for Christians, asking us to look in the present moment at whether we are creating heaven or hell for ourselves and others. What does God will for our lives, not just at the end of time, but all the time?

Bible Study Passages

Job 1:6–12; 2:1–10

Matt 25:31–46

Luke 16:19–31

Questions for Discussion

Share your understanding of heaven and hell.

Do you believe in heaven and hell?

What does the Bible say about heaven and hell?

---

9. St. Thomas's Church, including the Doom painting, is currently being repaired and renovated in 2020.

Should Christians believe in heaven and hell today?

Discuss the view that in the end all human beings will be saved by God.

Further Reading

Gooder, Paula. *Heaven*. London: SPCK, 2011.

Walls, Jerry L. *Heaven, Hell, and Purgatory: Rethinking the Things That Matter Most*. Grand Rapids: Brazos, 2015.

Afterword

LIVING FAITH: THROUGH THE Church's Year evolved from a perspective of three interlocking dimensions of experience: "living-moving world," "living-moving text," and "living-moving faith." That is to say, a sense that the whole of creation is alive and in motion, that the texts of the Bible come to life every time they're read, and that Christian faith in God is for ever growing and expanding in many different directions.

After using these reflections, you will, I am sure, have become aware of these different focal points. We cannot understand the dynamic reality of the universe if we continue to think of it in static terms and models. We cannot do justice to the rich and multilayered dimensions of the biblical texts if we imagine them to have a single fixed meaning, forever the same. And we cannot understand our own faith or grow in faith if we think Christianity is a set of facts simply waiting to be believed. No. All these things move along a continuum, weaving in and out of each other and feeding each other. This makes the business of preaching and teaching, meditating and reflecting, and growing and developing, an exciting and stimulating process. There's never a reason for faith to be boring, for we inhabit a world full of wonder.

I hope these fifty-two reflections have not only provided insightful studies when you were in a tight corner, but also that they have given you a different way of approaching things—a more exciting and engaging way of thinking of the world, listening to biblical texts, and imagining your faith. I hope that after working with them you will feel more at home with exploration in matters of theology and faith, more open perhaps to discovering new elements in traditional concepts than you did before. In addition to a sense of the dynamism of world, text, and faith, I hope you have also seen some of their interconnections.

As you have worked through the Christian year and dipped in and out of these pieces, I hope you will have come to re-appreciate the joys and wonders of thinking about the different ways that God comes to us, the joys of Christmas Cribs and Easter Gardens, of music and poetry, literature and paintings, fire and water, buildings and places, and of the lives of the saints. I hope you will have seen interconnections between things you had not connected before and found the perennial questions of humanity and divinity (and their relations) permeating diverse areas. There is no secular and sacred; it's all one world with many fundamental human and religious questions and insights appearing in contrary and dissimilar places. All this makes preaching and teaching, meditating, contemplating, and studying an exciting and joyful journey.

Above all, I hope that through these reflections you have found joy and growth in faith, and that you will continue to grow more deeply into the mystery we call God.

Bibliography

Attenborough, Richard, dir. *Shadowlands*. DVD. Hollywood: Paramount, 2005.
Augustine. *De Trinitate*. N.p.: Veritatis Splendor, 2012.
Barenboim, Daniel. *Everything Is Connected: The Power of Music*. London: Weidenfeld and Nicolson, 2008.
Barnard, John, et al., eds. *Ancient & Modern: Hymns and Songs for Refreshing Worship*. London: Hymns Ancient and Modern, 2013.
Batty, David, dir. *The Gospel of Mark*. DVD. London: Lion Hudson, 2014.
Bindley, T. Herbert, ed. *De Incarnatione Verbi Dei: Athanasius on the Incarnation*. Christian Classics series 3. N.p.: Leopold Classic Library, 2015.
Bond, Michael. *A Bear Called Paddington*. New York: HarperCollins, 2018.
Brown, Dan. *The Da Vinci Code*. New York: Doubleday, 2003.
Common Worship: Services and Prayers for the Church of England. London: Church House, 2000.
Cox, Brian, presenter. *The Planets*. DVD. London: BBC, 2019.
Dante. *The Divine Comedy 2: Purgatory*. Translated by Dorothy Sayers. London: Penguin, 1976.
Darwin, Charles. *The Origin of Species*. New York: Harper, 2011.
Eastwood, Clint, dir. *Jersey Boys*. DVD. Hollywood: Warner Bros., 2014.
Elliott, J. K. *The Apocryphal New Testament* Oxford: Oxford University Press, 1993.
Gardiner, John Eliot, dir. *The Creation*. With the Monteverdi Choir and the English Baroque Soloists. CD. Berlin: Deutsche Grammophon, 1996.
George, Andrew, trans. *The Epic of Gilgamesh*. London: Penguin, 2003.
Hawking, Stephen W. *Brief Answers to the Big Questions*. London: Murray, 2018.
———. *A Brief History of Time: From the Big Bang to Black Holes*. London: Bantam, 1988.
Hick, John, ed. *The Myth of God Incarnate*. London: SPCK, 1977.
Hurford, Peter, organist. *Bach: The Organ Works*. CD. London: Decca, 1995.
Irenaeus. *Against Heresies*. N.p.: Aeterna, 2016.
Isham, Gyles. *Rushton Triangular Lodge*. London: English Heritage, 2003.
King, Paul, dir. *Paddington & Paddington 2*. DVD. London: Studiocanal, 2018.
Kolodiejchuk, Brian, ed. *Mother Teresa: Come Be My Light*. London: Rider, 2008.

Bibliography

Lawrence, D. H. *Apocalypse*. London: Penguin, 1995.
Lean, David, dir. *Lawrence of Arabia*. DVD. Hollywood: Sony, 1989.
MacCulloch, Diarmaid. *A History of Christianity: The First Three Thousand Years*. London: Allen Lane, 2009.
———, presenter. *A History of Christianity*. DVD. London: BBC, 2010.
McGrath, Alister. *C. S. Lewis: A Life; Eccentric Genius, Reluctant Prophet*. London: Hodder and Stoughton, 2013.
Meeks, Wayne A., ed. *The HarperCollins Study Bible*. New Revised Standard Version. New York: Society of Biblical Literature, 1993.
Muggeridge, Malcolm. *Something Beautiful for God: Mother Teresa of Calcutta*. Oxford: Lion, 2009.
Myrone, Martin, and Amy Concannon. *William Blake*. Princeton: Princeton University Press, 2019.
Parrott, Andrew, dir. *Handel: Messiah*. With the Taverner Choir & Players. CD. London: Veritas, 1989.
Stillwater, Michael, dir. *Shining Night: A Portrait of the Composer Morten Lauridsen*. DVD. Santa Fe: Song Without Borders, 2012.
Tavener, John. *Innocence*. With the English National Orchestra and the Westminster Abbey Choir conducted by Martyn Neary. CD. CA: Sony, 1995.
Tertullian. *On Baptism*. Minnesota: Lighthouse, 2015.
Tillich, Paul. *Systematic Theology*. Vol. 2, pt. 111, *Existence and the Christ*. London: SCM, 1978.
Vaughan Williams, R., ed. *The English Hymnal*. Oxford: Oxford University Press, 1933.
Vermes, Geza. *The Complete Dead Sea Scrolls in English*. London: Penguin, 1997.
Wiesel, Elie. *Night*. London: Penguin, 2008.

www.ingramcontent.com/pod-product-compliance
Lightning Source LLC
Chambersburg PA
CBHW072135160426
43197CB00012B/2114